D0097740

EATING TOGETHER

Also by Lillian Hellman

Plays

THE CHILDREN'S HOUR (1934)

DAYS TO COME (1936)

THE LITTLE FOXES (1939)

WATCH ON THE RHINE (1941)

THE SEARCHING WIND (1944)

ANOTHER PART OF THE FOREST (1947)

MONTSERRAT (*An adaptation*, 1950)

THE AUTUMN GARDEN (1951)

THE LARK (*An adaptation*, 1956)

CANDIDE (*An operetta*, 1957)

TOYS IN THE ATTIC (1960)

MY MOTHER, MY FATHER AND ME (*An adaptation*, 1963)

THE COLLECTED PLAYS (1972)

Memoirs

AN UNFINISHED WOMAN (1969)

PENTIMENTO (1973)

SCOUNDREL TIME (1976)

THREE (*The collected memoirs, with new commentaries by the author*, 1979)

MAYBE (1980)

Editor of

THE SELECTED LETTERS OF ANTON CHEKHOV (1955)

THE BIG KNOCKOVER: SELECTED STORIES AND SHORT NOVELS OF DASHIELL HAMMETT (1966)

Also by Peter Feibleman

A PLACE WITHOUT TWILIGHT (1958)

THE DAUGHTERS OF NECESSITY (1959)

TIGER, TIGER BURNING BRIGHT (*A play*) (1963)

STRANGERS AND GRAVES (*Four novellas*) (1966)

THE COLUMBUS TREE (1973)

CHARLIE BOY (1980)

EATING TOGETHER

Recipes & Recollections

by LILLIAN HELLMAN
and PETER S. FEIBLEMAN

Little, Brown and Company · Boston · Toronto

FIRST EDITION

LIBRARY OF CONGRESS CATALOGING IN PUBLICATION DATA
Hellman, Lillian, 1906–
Eating together.

Includes index.
1. Cookery, International. 2. Cookery—Louisiana—New Orleans. 3. Hellman, Lillian, 1906– —Friends and associates. 4. Feibleman, Peter S., 1930– —Friends and associates. 5. Authors, American—20th century—Biography. I. Feibleman, Peter S., 1930– II. Title.
TX725.A1H36 1984 641.5 84-20173
ISBN 0-316-35508-9 (pbk.)

MV

Published simultaneously in Canada
by Little, Brown & Company (Canada) Limited

PRINTED IN THE UNITED STATES OF AMERICA

The authors wish to thank Molly O'Neill for her skill in testing the recipes in this book, and for her diplomacy in acting as culinary referee.

LH

PF

Contents

HER WAY

Lillian Hellman

1

ALL writers are lonely people and all writers are nervous people, particularly as they come to the end of a work. But Peter Feibleman takes the gold ring. I have lived around writers all my life and have never seen anything to match Peter's frantic nervousness as he finishes a book.

This was the case with *The Columbus Tree,* a good novel about Spain, that he finished in New Orleans in 1972.

I was so depressed and worried by the long-distance phone calls I was getting from him that I flew down to New Orleans to see what I could do. There was, of course, very little I could do, except to listen, and to listen was a horror: What, for example, should happen if the publishers (who had always published him) decided not to publish him? What, for example, would happen if the manuscript got lost going to the publisher? What, for example, would happen if he were shot the next day? (Although who besides myself would have done the shooting, I do not know.)

At the end of two or three days, I began to cry. This evidently touched Peter, who invited me to go to Brennan's for dinner. I was in such a state of nerves by this time from answering his numbskull questions, that three vodkas and half a bottle of wine went to my head. I was off to the ladies' room and on my way out afterward, I fell on a stone step, cut my knee very badly and was knocked unconscious for a minute or two.

People flew to get Peter, who came into the ladies' room, only to be told, by a lady dressed in a man's outfit, that he was in the wrong room.

He stopped bathing my wound long enough to say, "No, madam, but perhaps you are."

In any case, the book was eagerly accepted by the publishers, who sold it almost immediately to the Book-of-the-Month Club. Peter made some money. The book got good reviews. And so on. This story has a happy ending. But before it had a happy ending, it was decided to give him a publication party.

Now, publication parties are strange affairs. They can consist of your own friends, if you like, or they can consist of the influential part of the press, leaving out the rest, or they can be large enough for the entire press. The publishers and I decided on a small party of friends.

I cannot remember the guest list at this party, but I had it in my apartment and it was a Sunday lunch party. I always enjoy talking over a menu with someone I'm fond of — in this case, I telephoned my friend Hannah Weinstein, who happened to be in London producing a movie. When I told her that I couldn't decide on the right dessert, she didn't hesitate. "Chocolate cake," she said, "and use my recipe." So that was it, and I did, and it was wonderful.

Here are the recipes for the special occasion lunch to celebrate a publication.

FRESH SALMON MOUSSE

Serves 6

2 pounds fresh salmon
3 teaspoons salt
1 teaspoon white pepper
2 egg whites
1 cup sour cream
1 cup heavy cream, whipped to stiff peaks
green mayonnaise (recipe below)

Preheat oven to 350 degrees. Cut salmon into 1-inch pieces. Place salmon, salt, white pepper, egg whites and sour cream in the bowl of a food processor or blender. Blend until mixture is smooth and remove to a large bowl. Use a rubber spatula to gently fold in the whipped cream. Grease a tube pan mold generously with butter and fill with mousse mixture. Place mold in a baking pan and pour in boiling water to reach half the height of the mold. Bake at 350 degrees for 1½ hours or until the internal temperature of the mousse is 120 degrees.

Allow to cool, unmold, and serve with green mayonnaise.

GREEN MAYONNAISE

Yields about 1½ cups

1 cup spinach leaves, stems removed
10 leaves of fresh basil
1 clove of garlic
1 teaspoon salt
½ teaspoon pepper
pinch of cayenne pepper
3 egg yolks
2 tablespoons lemon juice
1½ cups olive oil
1 green onion, chopped

Boil spinach and basil leaves in plenty of water for 3 minutes. Drain and cool completely under cold water. Press leaves in a towel to dry, and set aside. Place garlic, egg yolks, salt and pepper in bowl of food processor or blender. Blend until egg yolks thicken slightly and begin to pale in color. Add lemon juice. Continue to blend and add oil in a slow, steady stream. When mixture has the consistency of a thick mayonnaise, add the spinach leaves, basil leaves and green onion. Blend until mixture is very green. Adjust seasoning with additional salt and a dash of cayenne pepper. Add hot water to achieve desired consistency.

STEAMED ASPARAGUS

Serves 6

2 bunches asparagus, woody ends cut off and tied in 6 bundles
½ lemon
hollandaise sauce (recipe below)

Cover the bottom of a tall pot with 1 inch of water and bring it to a boil. Stand asparagus bundles upright in pot. Add lemon, cover pot and steam until tender. Serve with hollandaise sauce.

HOLLANDAISE SAUCE

Yields 1 cup

3 egg yolks
3 tablespoons hot water
1½ tablespoons lemon juice
½ cup melted butter
dash of cayenne pepper
¼ teaspoon salt

In a double boiler whisk egg yolks over simmering water until they begin to thicken. Continue whisking while drizzling in hot water. Beat in lemon juice. Continue whisking and slowly drizzle butter into sauce. Season with cayenne pepper and salt to taste.

BRAISED QUAIL ON TOAST

Serves 6

12 quail
1 pound butter
1 cup white wine
salt and pepper
12 slices bread, crusts removed

Put the quail in a large pot with butter, wine and a little salt and pepper. Cover the pot and put it in a 350-degree oven for 15 minutes. Then take the pot out and put it on top of the stove. Brown an additional 5 minutes, turning once.

There is a very pleasant old-fashioned habit of serving quail on toast, in which case take the 12 slices of bread and toast them with the butter from the quail. Then put the quail on the toast, drizzle some more butter over, and serve.

STRAWBERRIES WITH GRAND MARNIER

Serves 6

2 pints strawberries, hulled and sliced
¼ cup Grand Marnier

Toss the strawberries with Grand Marnier about an hour before you plan to serve, and serve in wineglasses.

HANNAH WEINSTEIN'S CHOCOLATE CAKE

Yields 1 cake

¼ pound sweet butter, softened
½ cup granulated sugar
3 eggs, separated
12 ounces semisweet chocolate bits
3 tablespoons bourbon
1 teaspoon espresso coffee
⅓ cup almonds, ground
¼ teaspoon almond extract
¾ cup flour
pinch of salt

Preheat oven to 350 degrees. Cream the butter and sugar. In a separate bowl, beat egg yolks until thick and combine well with butter and sugar. In a small saucepan, melt chocolate, bourbon and espresso, and cool. Combine chocolate mixture with butter and sugar. Mix in almonds and almond extract. In a separate bowl, beat egg whites to stiff peaks. Alternate folding in flour and beaten egg whites until both are incorporated. Put batter in a greased and floured 8-inch cake pan and bake for 25 minutes. The center should be soft and the edges of the cake should be firm.

2

THIS book was conceived, in a sense, as a tribute to an old friendship. Peter and I first met when he was a child — a kind of old child — and I was a young woman. Through the years, we have become close friends and celebrated a great many holidays and special occasions together.

Perhaps because we were both born in New Orleans, we share a similar taste in foods, although his taste is more catholic than mine. He, for example, puts up with turkey, while I think it is worthless. He spent years in Spain and likes Spanish food. I do not.

The divergence has led me, in any case, to invent for myself, whenever we travel together, a way to eat, while leaving him alone.

Although many of our recipes have a foreign base, both of us are devoted to good American cooking; I, perhaps more than he, which may be my age, though I don't think so.

Nowadays, of course, with pre-cooked trash food and ready-to-heat TV dinners, good American cooking has been almost lost. There are still a few restaurants where it can be had, and a few homes where it is still practiced, but they are not many. So we have tried to include recipes for some of it, mixing them in with recipes from other lands.

You will note that we haven't always given exact timings, because there is no such thing in cooking. Exact timing cannot be done. It's a fake. It depends upon your stove, the pot you're cooking in, the temperature outside and too many other factors for any cookbook to tell you how long to do anything. Good cooking is chiefly common sense and good taste.

Take, for example, an American classic. There's very little better in this world than a well-baked Idaho potato, but it is usually offered to us underdone. Whenever this has happened to me, I've asked the cook or housewife how long he or she has baked it. The total given is somewhere around 30 to 35 minutes. This is just plain not long enough. A large Idaho must be baked for an hour. And it must not be cut into with any kind of knife. A knife does something bad, although we do not know why, to the steam coming from the baked potato.

It must be crushed open with the base of the hand, wrapped in a towel, so that the steam can pour out from several directions. When it has been crushed open enough, it can be pulled open a little further. A large pat of butter, salt and pepper should be placed within it and the steam allowed to melt the butter.

3

THERE is nothing better off the New England coast for eating than the mussels which cling to the rocks. They cost a good deal in fancy French restaurants, but on the rocks they are there for the picking.

Mussels are totally ignored — and I find this downright foolish — on the Cape and on my island, Martha's Vineyard, by the Portuguese or descendants of the Portuguese who came there originally to work on whaling ships. It is extremely interesting that the second-generation immigrant is, in most states of the union, unable to eat, or dislikes, the food found and made great use of by his father and grandfather.

(Perhaps one of the reasons for fine New Orleans cooking is the absence of such second-generation snobbery. The Cajuns fished, caught by nets, shot by gun, and ate exactly what their fathers had, and paid no attention to the fancified food of the city. Eventually, New Orleans itself found out how fine this food was, or could be, if it was properly cooked.)

If and when you pick mussels, you should wear a pair of thin gloves, because you will be putting your hands under water against hard rock. One very important precaution must be taken. The mussels must not be picked unless they are totally covered by water at all tides. In other words, you must not pick them up on beaches, nor from the top of rocks, where the sun could have got at them during the day.

Most important, you must make sure that the water is not

polluted. Mussels, like clams, can cause hepatitis. You should not eat lake or pond mussels that are striped.

But mussels are fun to pick. You will find them difficult to clean, but carry a thin iron pail or a canvas bucket with you, filled with salt water. Tear off the dirt and the stuff that clings to mussels as you go along.

When you get the mussels home, tear off some more of this muck and begin to scrape each one with the dull side of a table knife, until nothing is left on the top or bottom. Along the inner side of each mussel, you will find what is known as a beard. Tear off the beard with your fingers and drop the mussels in some cold salted water for half an hour. They are now ready for preparation.

Mussels can be eaten several ways, all of them delicious. Here are three recipes I am fond of:

MUSSELS MARINIÈRE

Serves 6

5 pounds mussels, cleaned and debearded
1 cup white wine
¼ pound butter
5 shallots, minced
1 cup parsley, minced

Put the mussels into the largest flat pot that you have; a 2-inch-deep iron pot is wonderful because it allows the steam to reach each mussel evenly. Add the wine and the shallots, butter and parsley. Cover the pot tightly and, over high heat, allow the mussels 3 or 4 minutes to open. Take care not to cook them too long, because they will toughen.

COLD MUSSELS MARINIÈRE

Prepare the mussels as above. When they are steamed open, strain them, save the liquid, and chill the mussels and broth in the refrigerator. To serve, take off half of the shell, leaving the mussel on the other side. Pour about ½ cup of the cold broth into a bowl, add 2 minced shallots, a tablespoon of vinegar and a tablespoon of olive oil. Mix very well and add a little chopped parsley. Pour a little of the dressing over each mussel and serve.

STEAMED MUSSELS

Serves 6

5 pounds mussels, cleaned and debearded
1 onion, sliced thin
1 teaspoon crushed red chili pepper
1 teaspoon black pepper
1 bay leaf
6 cups white wine
1 cup parsley, minced
1 lemon, quartered
1 tablespoon rosemary

Combine onion, crushed chili pepper, black pepper, bay leaf, wine, parsley, lemon and rosemary in a large pot and bring it to a boil. Add mussels, cover the pot, and steam until mussels are barely open. Pour mussels and sauce into a large bowl and serve.

WE have wonderful fish and shellfish in the waters surrounding America, particularly in the Atlantic. But shrimps, I feel, are now a waste of time and, since they are extremely expensive, a waste of your money, for unless you live in New Orleans or near a Gulf city, they have no taste whatsoever. They have been frozen too long and defrosted too much until they taste exactly like cardboard.

If you do live in a Gulf city, or in any city near shrimping waters, then that is something else and they are still wonderful.

But in ordinary recipes — the way New Orleans used to and probably still does cook shrimp (since the shrimp are still pretty good there) — there is no sense, it seems to me, in buying them at their current high price and ending up with a tasteless object.

MAINE LOBSTER

Maine lobsters are, I think, the best in the world. First, make sure they are alive, by seeing that they are kicking. Have ready a large pot, much larger than the largest lobster you are buying, and put it to boiling. Place in it some fresh dried red pepper or 4 or 5 drops of Tabasco sauce, 2 tablespoons of vinegar and 2 bay leaves, very finely crushed.

As soon as the water boils, put in the lobsters, head first. They will die immediately and mercifully. Put the lid on and cook them no more than 10 minutes. I have seldom cooked lobsters larger than 2 pounds, but I have found this 10-minute timing to work for the 2-pounders, as well as for the 1½-pounders. I thus suspect that you would only need 15 minutes for a 4-pound lobster. Usually, lobsters are overcooked.

If you wish to broil them, you will have to go to the fishmonger late in the day and have him cut in half what is called the tail, but should be called the body, unless you can do it with a very sharp knife or, perhaps, a cleaver. Stretch it open. Put dots of butter on it and put it under a very hot broiler. It needs nothing else but a little salt and pepper and, perhaps, a little melted butter at the very end of the broiling. The timing is the same.

BROILED BLUEFISH WITH MUSTARD MAYONNAISE

The reigning fish on my island is bluefish. The writer John Hersey (who is a great fisherman) and I have for years been fooling around with recipes for it. He does all kinds of brave things, such as making it in a Chinese fashion, but I can only make it in one fashion:

Filet the bluefish, or have it fileted. Place in a broiling pan, skin side down. Rub the meat side with a little salt and pepper and some mayonnaise with a little mustard mixed in (recipe follows). The mustard lubricates the fish and keeps it from drying out. Put it under the broiler and be careful not to broil it too much. The filets from an average bluefish (that weighs 5 or 6 pounds) take no more than 10 or 12 minutes to broil.

Mustard Mayonnaise

2 egg yolks
1½ teaspoons lemon juice
½ teaspoon salt
pinch of cayenne pepper
1 teaspoon Dijon mustard
1 teaspoon dry mustard
1 cup olive oil
2 tablespoons boiling water

Beat egg yolks to thicken slightly. Add lemon juice, salt, cayenne pepper and mustard and combine. Continue beating mixture and add oil drop by drop. When all oil has been added, add boiling water. The boiling water stabilizes the mayonnaise while thinning it to a smooth consistency. Adding oil too quickly will cause the mayonnaise to "break" — the oil separates and the mixture becomes a runny mess. If this happens, simply remove the mixture from the mixing bowl. Begin with an additional egg yolk, mustard, salt and pepper. Slowly introduce the original mixture to repair the mayonnaise.

BONITO

We also have a great deal of bonito. One can either cut it into steaks of about 1 inch thick, and broil them, preferably over charcoal, or prepare with the above recipe for bluefish.

BLUE CRABS

Once upon a time, we had many hard-shell crabs much like the blue crabs of New Orleans, which are, I think, my favorite of all shellfish. But on my island, they seem to have disappeared. They must also have disappeared in many parts of America, since the price has risen greatly in the markets. But, if you can find some, they are very good indeed. Although they are trouble to eat, crabs are a good deal better when cooked in the shell.

Put the live crabs in the sink and turn on the cold water. Have ready a large pair of tongs. Put on the stove a large pot of boiling water in which you have crushed 2 or 3 dried hot red peppers or 4 or 5 drops of Tabasco, along with 1 cut-up onion, 1 clove of garlic, a fair amount of crushed bay leaves and 2 tablespoons of vinegar.

Crabs have little flavor and must be highly seasoned. In New Orleans, they are often boiled in beer, but now, that seems extravagant. If you have an extra bottle of beer around, put the beer in the water and bring the water to a boil.

When the crabs are kicking in the cold water, bring the pot over to the sink. Pick up the crabs carefully with the tongs and drop them into the boiling water. They will die almost immediately.

When all the crabs are in the pot, return the pot to the stove and cook the crabs for 8 to 10 minutes. As soon as they are cooked, remove them from the water and let them cool.

Shelling a crab sounds more difficult than it is. Put it on its back. You will see that there is a place to put your finger under the shell. Lift it up gently and the whole back will begin to move. Tear off the back and crack the crab in half. Along each side is a kind of inedible material which is spongy and rather triangular in shape. Remove it. This is very simple to do. The crab is now ready to eat, or for use in the New Orleans dish, gumbo.

If the crab is female, you may be lucky and find coral in the shell. Carefully remove this with a spoon and keep it to one side. It is very good.

CRAB GUMBO

Serves 6

3 dozen crabs
3 tablespoons brown roux (see recipe page 112)
1 onion, minced
1 green pepper, minced
2 cloves garlic, minced
2 pounds okra, sliced small
½ cup parsley, minced
1 bay leaf
½ teaspoon thyme
¼ teaspoon cayenne pepper
¼ teaspoon white pepper
¼ teaspoon black pepper
5 tomatoes, peeled, seeded and chopped

Boil and pick the crabs. Save 8 cups of broth. Melt roux in a large skillet. Add onion, green pepper, garlic, okra, parsley, bay leaf, thyme and pepper, and cook for 3 minutes. Add tomatoes and reserved crab broth and simmer for 1 hour. Add crabmeat, cook for 15 more minutes, and serve.

I WAS in Los Angeles and saw Peter Feibleman not long after Dorothy Parker died. I knew that she had been very fond of him and lived near him and I wanted to hear any stories he had about her.

He took me to what is still, I think, the best restaurant in Los Angeles, Perino's, a long way from Hollywood, toward downtown Los Angeles and for some reason I cannot understand, rather snubbed by movie people. Perhaps because it is elegant and quiet, has lovely, comfortable seats and isn't full of other people like themselves.

I remember the evening very well, because I had such a nice time and I roared so over Peter's stories about Parker, one of which I used as an end to the piece I wrote about her in my book *An Unfinished Woman.* I also remember a wonderful dish that we had that night.

SAUTÉED VEAL WITH MUSHROOMS AND LEMON SAUCE

Serves 6

12 medallions (½ inch thick) ribeye veal
flour
salt and pepper

½ cup butter
2 cups mushrooms, sliced thin
¼ cup lemon juice
½ cup chicken broth
1 cup heavy cream

Dust the veal medallions with flour and season with salt and pepper. Melt the butter and sauté the veal. Brown on both sides and remove from pan. Add the mushrooms and season lightly with salt and pepper. Cook for 5 minutes over moderate heat until mushrooms soften. Add lemon juice and chicken broth and scrape the pan well. Add cream and simmer over low heat until thick. Taste and add more salt or pepper if needed. Spoon sauce over the veal and serve.

This dish should be served with fresh steamed asparagus or buttered noodles or both.

ONE November, Peter and I were foolish enough to go to a motel in Palm Springs. The weather was cold, and it was the shabbiest motel I think I've ever been in. Maybe the pool, in which we didn't swim, was shabbier than any of the rest of it.

But our friend Max Palevsky was staying in his beautiful house there and was kind enough to take us to a restaurant where we had a dinner that was so good, I think of it as an alternate for Thanksgiving, although it can be a dinner for any nice winter night, when you are having guests whom you truly like and whom you wish to spend some money on. Treat yourself to some very good red wine with it.

LEG OF VENISON

Serves many

2 cups red wine
2 shallots, minced
2 cloves garlic, minced
2 tablespoons Worcestershire sauce
1 teaspoon thyme
1 teaspoon poultry seasoning
2 tablespoons black pepper
1 leg of venison
½ cup cream

Combine wine, shallots, garlic, Worcestershire sauce, thyme, poultry seasoning and black pepper. Make cuts in the venison and push into the cuts additional thinly sliced shallots and occasional pieces of thinly sliced garlic. Rub the venison with salt and pepper and let it stand in the marinade for 24 hours, basting frequently with the marinade.

No absolute timing can be given for the roasting. It depends (a) upon your stove, whether it's electric or gas, and (b) upon how you like venison. If you like it very well done, it will take at least 25 to 30 minutes per pound. If you like it medium rare, it will take 15 to 18 minutes per pound. If you like it really rare, which is not recommended, you will need 10 to 12 minutes per pound.

Bake it in a 350- to 375-degree oven and do not let the marinade evaporate. If necessary, add a little water. When it is nearly finished, pour in ½ cup of cream and move it to the top of the stove. Swish the gravy around, being careful not to sour the cream. Slice it carefully into thin slices and serve with a slightly tart vegetable, such as turnips, brussels sprouts, or sweet and sour cabbage.

SWEET AND SOUR CABBAGE

1 head cabbage, cored and cut into eight parts
2 tablespoons butter
1 clove garlic, minced
1 onion, chopped
1 tablespoon vinegar
1 tablespoon sugar
1 cup raisins

Steam the cabbage until it is well done. In the meantime, melt the butter in a big iron pan. Add a large chopped onion and the garlic. From this point, the taste has to be yours. I start with 1 tablespoon of vinegar and 1 bare tablespoon of sugar. Now, taste it. It will either be too sour or too sweet. It is never right on the first taste. Keep on tasting until you find the proper balance of sweetness and sourness. Add a handful of raisins and let them bubble around until they fluff up. Toss the cabbage in the sauce for about 5 minutes. The same sauce, incidentally, is very good for string beans.

Have with this dinner a mixture of sherbets (lemon and pineapple mix very well) and a nice piece of cake that isn't too heavy. That is all that is needed.

Another fine winter meal especially around Christmastime is roast goose. I use two different stuffings in two different geese to serve ten people. Both of them are delicious.

ROAST GOOSE

Geese begin to come in this time of the year and, if you have a good butcher, it is possible they will not be frozen. But if they are, it does not make that much difference. Let them defrost in the refrigerator.

Wash the geese thoroughly inside and out, salt and pepper them inside and out and let them stand in the bottom of the refrigerator for one day. By this time, the extra fat which usually grows around the bottom of the goose can be cut off. Please save it and put it to one side. It is very valuable. Do not cut too much of the fat off, because you will need some to sew up for the dressing.

One of the stuffings I use is made of oysters, and the other is made of mashed potatoes with scallions. Which dressing you use should be to your taste, and the time of roasting the geese should not vary with the dressing you use. Five or ten minutes one way or the other is not worth worrying about.

Oyster Dressing

2 cups breadcrumbs
1 tablespoon bourbon
2 tablespoons milk
1 onion, minced
2 tablespoons butter
1 pint shucked oysters with liquor
2 teaspoons salt
1 teaspoon pepper

I suggest using Pepperidge Farm dressing for the breadcrumbs. Mix the dressing well with bourbon and milk and knead it until it is moist. Sauté the onion until it is soft and add it to the mixture. Add the oysters and as much liquor as needed — you wish to come out with something moist, but not too moist, and it must be firm in order to stay put properly.

Add salt and pepper until the dressing has a pleasant flavor. Stuff the goose and use a trussing needle to go through the skin of the goose and take small skewers and put them through one side and then the other, pulling a heavy thread around each skewer until it is firmly in place and the dressing cannot emerge. But do not sew or truss too tightly, because the dressing will explode all over the pan.

Mashed Potato and Scallion Dressing

10 medium-size potatoes, cleaned and peeled
3 tablespoons butter
1 tablespoon heavy cream
1 tablespoon salt
1½ teaspoons pepper
1 bunch scallions, including green tops, chopped

Boil the potatoes until they are soft and put them through a potato masher. Add butter, cream and salt and pepper. Stir in the scallions. Stuff the goose as instructed above. The extra dressing is good all by itself, so keep it warm for dinner.

Cooking the Geese

Put the geese in a 350-degree oven, counting roughly 2½ to 3 hours, and perhaps longer, depending on the quality or the age of the geese. You can only make sure of this by putting a fork to the legs and seeing if the juice runs clear. For the last ½ hour, turn the stove up to 450 degrees. Turn the geese on one side and then the other and let them brown and crisp. There will now be a great deal of fat in the pan. Do not baste with the fat, but pour a little hot water over the geese if you need to. (Save the fat from the pan. It is very valuable for cooking other things.)

When the geese have cooled, carve them, removing the legs first and cutting the leg from the thigh and working down, to get even slices of the rest. The wings of the goose are not worth much, but if they are crisp enough, they are nice to chew on.

I do not believe that goose should have a first course. The dinner becomes too large and heavy. Serve with it some finely mashed turnips, or some nicely cooked brussels sprouts. Have a beet and endive and walnut salad (see page 71) and a lemon and pineapple sherbet (see page 36). Have some cookies if you wish them, but they are not necessary.

ONE of my most vivid childhood memories is of my third birthday party, where, I guess, every child in the school and in the neighborhood had been asked to come. (I was not consulted about the guest list.)

Suddenly, I, in theory the hostess, dressed in a very frilly dress made by the nuns in New Orleans, decided to go sit in a corner with my cat. There were outcries from my mother, my aunts and my nurse: I was ruining my dress, the corner was dirty, what was the matter with me, why was I crying, why was I holding the cat, why didn't I get up and stand waiting like a proper little lady?

But the more they said, the more I bawled. The demands, then the orders, then the threats, got nobody anywhere. I'm told that the more they spoke, the more I screamed. I squeezed the cat tighter and tighter.

The whole scene grew so loud that my tall, beloved grandmother, who was six feet two, appeared on the balcony of the living room and spoke a few sentences that I have remembered all my life. She said it to her own daughters.

She said, "Leave the child alone. We each have our own troubles and age has nothing to do with it. And leave the cat alone. He has his troubles. Why don't you all go eat some ice cream?"

I remember looking up at her with more love and gratitude than I was to feel again for many years.

I won whatever silly victory I was out to get, because I never rose from the floor during the entire party, until the cat scratched me so badly from the pain of my holding him that they carried me to my father's room to clean the wounds.

My beautiful dress was splotched with iodine and on my face was a crisscross of ugly marks and bruises. My dress was torn off my shoulders. I have a picture of myself, still looking angry, which was taken twenty-four hours later, evidently by someone witty, perhaps my grandmother. Of course, it took me a week to get over the indignity of being asked to join my own birthday party. The expression seems to have lasted for the camera.

A hand can be vaguely seen in this picture; it is the hand of my beloved nurse, Sophronia, who was holding me and telling me to behave. Perhaps I am not the right person to ask for advice on children's birthday parties.

But my sixteenth birthday was a charmer. My father allowed me to choose the place and I picked the hotel roof where Paul Whiteman and his band were playing.

This time I was allowed to have all the boys and girls I liked until three o'clock in the morning. It was an era of some very strange dancing. One of the oddities was that the boy, whirling the girl around the floor, had to hold her by the waist while she leaned the upper part of her body backwards as far as it would go. It was a kind of gym-dance trick, and it looked very ugly, but it felt very nice.

I don't remember what anybody else wore, but I had a pretty dress from Paris, France, made of a gold-shot satin material with gold fringe at the hem, which I carried through college with me and which was on loan almost every weekend and worn so often that it finally disintegrated.

A sixteenth or eighteenth birthday is a nice occasion, but I am not sure it should be given at home unless you have a home big enough for a small band. It is pleasant for young people to dance, and if your house is big enough, do it there.

If you do it at home, I suggest this menu: a big lobster salad, cold roast chicken, French bread, ambrosia, champagne or dry white wine.

LOBSTER SALAD

You will boil the number of lobsters appropriate to the number of people you are feeding. Two 2-pound lobsters, with claws carefully removed, feed about three persons.

Oddly enough, very large lobsters take little more time to boil than 3-pound lobsters. In any case, if the lobster weighs more than 5 pounds, cook it for 20 minutes; cook a 3-pound lobster for 15 minutes.

Have ready a large pot of boiling water in which you have crushed 2 or 3 bay leaves. Put in some salt and red pepper. Put the lobster in immediately and it will die very fast.

Take it out of the water after it is cooked and let it cool. When it is cool enough to handle, either slit the body (if that is the right term) or if you are careful, you can pull the body away from the head and pull the meat from the body in one piece.

Crack the claws and remove the meat. Take the coral, if any, off the lobster, removing the head. Add to the lobster meat.

Chop the meat into small pieces and, depending on the size of the lobster or lobsters, take a medium or large purple or sweet onion and put it through a food chopper.

Make some homemade mayonnaise (recipe below). Using about ¼ to ½ cup of good French dressing, mix the mayonnaise into the bowl of French dressing. Mix the lobster, onion and dressing together, taking care not to crush the lobster. Take a spare tablespoon of capers and mix through the lobster meat.

Save enough dressing to surround the lobster meat and top the lettuce. Separately place one-quarter of a hard-boiled egg per person on the lettuce, decorated with a little dressing and a caper or two.

HOMEMADE MAYONNAISE

3 egg yolks
2 cups olive oil
½ teaspoon salt
½ teaspoon pepper
1 tablespoon lemon juice
boiling water

Most books are very strict about mayonnaise. This is nonsense. I once had a very great cook, unhappily now dead, who made almost twice the mayonnaise I could make with the same amount of oil and eggs. I have found, however, that I cannot do with less than 3 egg yolks and 2 cups of either olive oil, Wesson oil, or peanut oil. Olive oil is, of course, the better-tasting oil.

Begin by putting a kettle of water on to boil. Fill a baster with the oil, put the eggs in a bowl, and whip them slightly. Add the salt and pepper immediately and start blending the mixture with an electric beater. Begin adding the oil from the baster, drop by drop. (This is the only strict rule for making mayonnaise. You must, at the very first of the process, go very slowly.) Continue beating with the electric beater and adding drops of oil. When you have used over half of the oil, the mixture will be a thick consistency. Stop beating and taste the mayonnaise. Begin adding lemon juice. I find that about half a lemon, if it is very juicy, is more than enough. But add the lemon juice to your taste. Then go back and add the remaining olive oil, with the baster. The mixture will become very thick.

Fill a soup spoon with water from the kettle and add to the mayonnaise. Beat it once more and it is finished.

ROAST CHICKEN

Take the chicken out of the icebox 5 or 6 hours before you are ready to cook it. Wipe the chicken well on the outside and the inside. Put some salt and pepper on the outside. Cut an onion into quarters.

Place it inside the chicken, along with one piece of garlic and some tarragon. Sprinkle a fair amount of tarragon on the outside, rubbing it in with some salt and butter. Start in a 400-degree oven, and, depending on the size of the chicken, roast it for 1 to 2 hours, turning up the heat at the end to make it nice and crisp.

Cut the chicken delicately and decorate it with watercress.

Start the party with some champagne, but do not continue with champagne, because it is too expensive. Substitute a good, dry white wine, which can go all through dinner, as well as after.

If you have a large enough place for musicians, you have a large enough table for almost everybody to sit down. This room can also be set up with small tables, which is an even nicer idea. If you have the party in a hotel, the lobster will be, of course, much too expensive, so see what menus you can arrange with the hotel, but go in a day before and ask to taste what they have fixed. Usually, hotel food is dreadful.

7

SPECIAL occasions change as you grow older: birthday parties are not as frequent as other special events. After-theater buffet suppers were a frequent occasion in my home.

Since few people have servants who will cook or remain until midnight, it is best to fix a buffet supper yourself beforehand, and have several dishes for people to choose from. Here are four:

DECENT SCRAMBLED EGGS

Serves 8

8 eggs
1 tablespoon water
1 teaspoon salt
½ teaspoon pepper
1 tablespoon chives
1 tablespoon parsley, minced
4 tablespoons butter

Break the eggs in a large bowl and beat hard. Add water, salt, pepper, chives and parsley. Melt the butter in an iron pan. When it is thoroughly melted, pour in the eggs and get ready to stand in front of the stove. Begin to beat the minute your eggs cook. A wooden spoon is best. You must continue this beating until the eggs have reached a nice, soft consistency. (There is nothing to my mind worse than hard scrambled eggs. They taste like last year's calendar.) Have a large platter warm and ready, and the minute the eggs have settled to the right consistency, put them on the platter and sprinkle them with additional chives.

KIPPERS

They are getting hard to find, but they can be found: kippers without tomato sauce.

Open the can and you will find that each kipper is divided by paper. Take a large iron pan and put in 1 tablespoon of butter. Let the butter melt and begin to remove the kippers from the can. Once in the pan, let each side of the kipper warm thoroughly. Take two spatulas and carefully turn each kipper. Put the kippers on a heated platter and serve them, leaving the spatula on the platter for people to use to serve themselves.

CHICKEN LIVERS

Serves 8

½ cup sweet butter
1 onion, minced
2 teaspoons salt
1 teaspoon black pepper
4 pounds chicken livers
3 tablespoons vermouth
2 tablespoons vinegar
2 tablespoons parsley, minced

Chicken livers must come from a first-class store because they must be absolutely fresh. Melt the butter in a pan and cook the onion until it is soft and gray. Season the chicken livers with salt and pepper and soak them in the vermouth. When the onion is soft, add the chicken livers. Brown them on each side. Add the vermouth and vinegar and let the whole thing bubble up. Chicken livers should not cook more than 3 or 4 minutes — just until they are no longer rare. If the sauce needs a little more vinegar or vermouth, add it. Keep the chicken livers hot on the back of the stove and serve on a platter. The livers can be combined with the scrambled eggs, but I think that is wasteful since they make a fine dish by themselves.

CHICKEN HASH

Serves 8

1 fowl
¼ pound sweet butter
¼ cup brandy
2 onions, minced
2 tablespoons parsley, minced
pinch of thyme
¼ cup heavy cream
¼ cup grated Parmesan cheese

Simmer the fowl in enough water to cover, for 2 hours. Remove the bird and allow to cool and save the broth for later use. Take all the skin off the chicken and chop the meat into very small pieces. Take a large pan, add the butter, and let it bubble up. Add the onions and cook them until they are gray and soft. Add the brandy. Add the chicken, parsley, thyme and heavy cream. When the mixture has bubbled up, transfer it to a casserole, sprinkle with Parmesan cheese, and place under the broiler until the cheese is golden brown.

As you can see, all these dishes have to be done at the last minute. But if you prepare the ingredients first, it will not take you very long to cook them and they will all be ready at the same time.

Put them on the buffet table and, if you are very generous, have a green salad. What is necessary is a loaf of hot French bread, cut and buttered.

BOTH Peter Feibleman and I were born in New Orleans, although, God knows, in different years, as he is usually eager to point out. But I don't mind that, since I have discovered that all men in their forties like to dine with women older than themselves, and to sleep with women much younger than themselves. (The two go hand in hand.)

A few years ago, we were both invited back to our native city to give lectures before the New Orleans Public Library organization. I was also invited to attend a Tulane University function in which I was to be given an honorary degree. This was pleasant, because Tulane University, as well as New Orleans, had not, as far as I can remember, ever acknowledged the fact that I was alive, and certainly had ignored me since I appeared before the House Un-American Activities Committee in 1952.

A small party joined Peter and me on our journey to New Orleans, to attend the lectures or to enjoy the food, or just because they had nothing else to do: Max and Linda Palevsky and Claudette Colbert.

I should mention an incident that took place at one of my lectures, when I realized, I suppose for the first time, how much of my eyesight was really lost. I was sitting on the stage at a table with a lamp on it and a lamp behind me, reading from "Julia" and smoking, with a package of Kleenex next to me.

About ten feet away was the president's stand-in. (The president himself was on a plane that had been delayed because of a storm and the dean was taking his place on the platform.)

I had, for some reason, taken a dislike to the dean; perhaps because he had rearranged my lamps at the last minute. In any case, I suddenly felt a hand close over mine and somebody pounding on the table. I was convinced that it was the dean, who had taken away my cigarettes and my drink. I thought, "I will wait until this lecture is finished to have it out with that idiot."

I finished reading and was waiting to see the dean, when I was pushed into a rather long car by Claudette and Peter. In the car I said, "Did you see that son of a bitch put out my cigarette and take my glass of Scotch away from me?"

Claudette said, "That son of a bitch was Peter. Don't you know what you did? You set the Kleenex on fire. Peter jumped on the stage, put his hand on the fire and put it out for you. And so did President Hackney's wife. You must thank her. But Peter got there first." She added, "You almost emptied the hall." I started to laugh and Claudette said, "Lilly, it may not be your eyes; it may be that you are going crazy. Didn't you smell it? If there's something the matter with your eyes, that doesn't excuse your nose."

I said no, I didn't smell it and I didn't believe the story. Well, the story was true. Peter *had* jumped on the stage and I had *not* smelled the fire. I guess the place was about to be emptied.

In any case, on to the gumbo. Peter and I have different memories of gumbo. Mine start with my aunt's boardinghouse, where it was cooked every Sunday, along with crayfish bisque. I was not allowed to play until I had helped the cook, who was, indeed, a wonderful cook, as was my Aunt Jenny. My job was to peel the shrimp, or the crayfish for crayfish bisque or to do whatever small thing could be trusted to a child.

Many, many years later, when I lived with Hammett, we were very broke and I amended this recipe, because we couldn't afford the shrimps, nor the crabs, nor much of anything. We used the vegetables that were growing in the garden of the rented house we had on Long Island and would add only a piece of ham. It really wasn't bad. If you have a garden and a good piece of highly smoked ham, try it. But the good piece of ham, you do need.

To return to my trip to New Orleans with Peter. The most pleasant part of it happened on the morning we were to leave. I was closing my valises. A tall, young, handsome black man was waiting for me in the lobby of the hotel.

He immediately put out his hand and said, "You are Miss Hellman. I recognize you. My name is Carl."

I said, "Hello, Carl."

He said, "You knew my grandmother. She used to cook in your aunt's boardinghouse and she has nice memories of you as a little girl."

I reached up to kiss him. He was such a pleasant memory of his grandmother.

He looked rather embarrassed in the lobby, but he said, "Miss Hellman, I have brought you something from my grandmother and I hope it's no trouble for you to take on the plane."

He had two very large plastic containers of gumbo, all taped and ready for me to carry on the plane, surrounded by ice. It was just as good a gumbo as I remembered from my childhood. The darling Brennan sisters have often sent me some from their fine restaurant, the Commander's Palace.

This is my recipe. Peter's will appear in his part of the book. I advise you to follow his, since he cooks it better than I do, but mine is easier. He makes a roux; I do not because I always burn it and it worries me. But there is a right way to make it and it is in Peter's recipe.

GUMBO FOR SIX

2 pounds okra
¼ cup bacon fat
1 10-ounce can of plum tomatoes, drained
1 ham hock
1 tablespoon salt
1 small hot pepper, minced
1½ teaspoons Worcestershire sauce
1 teaspoon Tabasco sauce
2 onions, minced
2 cloves garlic, minced
2 bay leaves
pinch of thyme
pinch of oregano
pinch of basil
1½ pounds shrimp
2 chicken legs
2 chicken thighs
6 oysters
1 cup converted rice

Cut off each end of each piece of okra and sauté for about 5 minutes in some bacon fat. Transfer okra to a large pot and keep bacon fat aside.

Add a large can of Italian plum tomatoes, having thrown off the juice from the can. Put in a highly smoked ham hock. Start the mixture on a high flame and turn it to simmer. Put in some salt, the hot pepper, a little Worcestershire sauce and a little Tabasco sauce.

Cut 1 large or 2 medium-size onions very fine and sauté them in the same bacon fat you have used for the okra (add more if necessary) until it is slightly gray.

Then, add it to the tomatoes and ham hock. Add 2 finely minced cloves of garlic into the mixture. Put in 2 crushed bay leaves, a pinch of thyme, a pinch of oregano, and a pinch of basil. Start the boil again, then turn to simmer.

When it has cooked for about an hour, taste it and correct the seasoning. In the meantime, shell 1½ pounds of shrimp, and put the shells in ½ cup of water with a little salt and pepper. Bring that water to a boil, simmer for 15–20 minutes, strain it and add the shrimp broth to the tomato mixture. Taste the tomato mixture once again for seasoning and possible correction. You can add pieces of slightly browned chicken; add the raw oysters taken from their shells with their liquid. Let the pot simmer again for about ½ hour without the cover. It should be thickened; the okra should have done it. If not, use arrowroot or some cornstarch mixed in a cup of liquid from the pot until smooth (no lumps), and add it to the tomato mixture.

You are now about ½ hour from being finished with the gumbo, so it is time to wash as much rice as you need, so it will be done and dry when the gumbo is finished.

Rice can be dried in several ways. If you use 1 cup of rice and 2½ cups of water, let it boil and do not remove the cover. When you think it is done (20–25 minutes), remove the cover. If it is not dry, place the rice in a colander in a 300-degree oven and it will dry out soon enough.

Back to the gumbo: New Orleans actually serves this heavy dish as a soup. I think this is a great mistake. It should be served as a main dish.

Put into your soup plates a large tablespoon of rice. Ladle the gumbo around it and on top of it. The idea is to give your guests the idea, if they haven't got sense enough, to mix the two.

Have a simple lettuce salad with the gumbo and follow it with a sherbet, the one you like best. I like pineapple and lemon. Here is a home recipe for it from my friend Lady Keith.

PINEAPPLE LEMON ICE

Serves 6

1¾ cups water
1¾ cups sugar
1 ripe pineapple, peeled and chopped
juice of 1 lemon
rind of 1 lemon, minced

Bring to boil the water and sugar. Boil slowly for 3 minutes and cool. Puree the pineapple in a food processor or blender. Add this puree to the syrup mixture along with the juice and rind of 1 lemon. Freeze in a 1-quart container of an ice-cream freezer, or if no ice-cream freezer is available, place the mixture in a large bowl in the freezer of your refrigerator. Allow to freeze for 4 hours, stirring frequently.

To unmold, dip only once in warm water. Invert onto a large plate. If the mold does not come out, let it sit at room temperature for a few minutes. Do not return to warm water or it will melt too fast.

9

ABOUT seven or eight years ago, Peter and I went to a rummy town called Puerto Vallarta, Mexico, and stayed in a rather grand-looking, second-rate hotel, where Peter, who loves room service and can eat terrible food as long as it is delivered to the room, happily ate bad hamburgers for two weeks.

I do not like hamburgers. I do not like rummy towns. I finally wandered around the town enough to buy myself one can of sardines, one can of very inferior salmon, a bottle of olive oil, a small bottle of vinegar, some crackers, some tea, some eggs and a sterno stove. I made tea on the sterno stove in a 25-cent pot and ate the bare sardines on crackers and made the not-too-bad salmon into salad, with an egg boiled on the sterno stove.

My meals were certainly not a feast. They were not even good, but they were a hell of a lot better than what Peter was eating and I knew we weren't staying long, anyway. It was nice to swim with the dolphins off the rocks, slightly beyond the hotel. I would swim in and among them and wonder whether anybody had ever eaten dolphin and how it would taste and what miserable man would ever kill them.

I thought that if I got too hungry, maybe I would be the miserable man who would, so one day, I went back to tell Peter that I couldn't stay any longer. We moved on to Mexico City, which is a splendid city, but Mexican food is not to my taste, I am afraid, or is not to my taste in Mexico.

I've had wonderful Mexican food in the house of Donna O'Neill in California on the great O'Neill ranch and I have had wonderful Mexican food cooked by a great New Orleans chef, but this was my fifth visit to Mexico and I've never had good food there.

10

I SPENT a good deal of my early twenties in Paris, staying for a long time when I was first married and Arthur Kober and I were on our honeymoon. He had a job on a magazine and I would write bad short stories in a dollar-a-day room on the rue Jacob.

The franc was very low in those days and one ate well on fifty cents a day. I particularly remember a great little restaurant called the Fourth Republic — way ahead of its time in name — and way behind its time in food. But it was good, decent food in a nice, old-fashioned way. They made the best lamb stew I think I've ever eaten, before or after. I have tried to find the restaurant many times since, but I think it's long gone out of business. But here is the lamb stew as I got it from the owner when I first went to the restaurant.

LAMB STEW RESTAURANTE FOURTH REPUBLIC

Serves 6

1 pound lamb, cut into 1-inch chunks
flour
¼ cup bacon fat
2 cups chicken stock
2 teaspoons salt
1 teaspoon pepper
¼ teaspoon oregano

1 clove garlic, minced
½ teaspoon thyme
2 bay leaves
1 teaspoon Worcestershire sauce
3 carrots, peeled and cut into thirds
3 small onions, peeled and cut in half
¼ cup rye

Dust the pieces of lamb with flour and brown them in bacon fat. Add chicken broth, salt and pepper, oregano, garlic, thyme, bay leaves and Worcestershire sauce. Bring to a boil and simmer for 2 hours. Add more chicken stock if necessary, to barely cover the lamb. After one hour, add the carrots and onions. In the last ½ hour of cooking, add the rye. Serve with homemade noodles (recipe follows).

It is wise to make more of this stew than you need. It freezes fine and is good to have in the house.

FRESH NOODLES

3½ cups semolina flour
1 tablespoon salt
4 eggs

Combine flour and salt. Mix the eggs together in a separate bowl. Place flour and salt on a board, form a well in the center, and pour in eggs. Quickly combine flour, salt and eggs. Add more flour if necessary, and knead dough until it is satiny smooth. Allow to rest in refrigerator for one hour. Roll dough on a lightly floured surface until it is an even thickness and almost translucent. Sprinkle dough with flour and roll into a loose cylinder. Use a sharp knife to cut noodles into the desired width. Cook in boiling water until noodles are cooked through.

It was that year in Paris when I met Janet Flanner, who lived not far away and who had her favorite restaurant, which was called Antoine's. It was very near my favorite restaurant, so we switched back and forth a good deal.

And it was that year in Paris when I first met Louis Aragon

and Phillipe Soupault, who later became my close friends, although they did not always stay close to each other.

It was fun to hear about the beginnings of Dadaism and it was my first real knowledge of Picasso. I guess my first real knowledge of many things came from either or both of them. I was not conscious of it, but I think most of the world we know now started around that time, and while I was no part of it, since I had done nothing, I was there to see a little piece of it and to appreciate it and I'm grateful for that.

What talented men and women they were — all of them. I clearly remember how jealous I was of their knowledge and their brilliance and how inferior I felt. I didn't meet too many people, really, although I'm always now appearing in books as having been met by somebody or other, but in the 1920's, I really didn't. I was, in fact, too young and too unknown to be bothered with by most, but Aragon, Soupault and Janet liked me and that was fine.

This is not to say that past times were better than now. I am no admirer of the past, except in a very few matters and for a very few people. The world has advanced, although some of the advances are ugly. But even if we come down to something as low as the vacuum cleaner, we realize that it's a big step away from a broom and mop and one's knees. Modern medicine is certainly better than the medicine of the 1920's and 1930's, although it's not worth a war to have it better.

But the 1920's were, I think, a period of great creativity. I guess it has always happened that way after a war. The Greeks and the Romans in all their wars have proved it. It goes in a circle and always has, like a child's dance of ring-around-the-rosy. If I am any good, the person holding my hand has a chance of being even better.

And so, whatever reservations we now have about Hemingway (Hammett and I always had many reservations), he deserves credit for the vigor and the sweep and the trying for something new. We now, of course, underrate Hemingway as we once overrated him, and that's in the cards for probably everybody who ever creates anything.

In any case, the year that we spent on the rue Jacob in the dollar-a-day room, worrying, was the only year I ever liked Paris.

I do not go back to Paris anymore. My last long visit was the year Simone Signoret produced and translated and acted in and directed and I think made the costumes and did the makeup and painted the theater and took the tickets, for a production of *The Little Foxes*.

Miss Signoret and I did not get along. I did not like her translation and it had not been the original agreement between us that she would do the translation by herself. I also did not like her as a stage actress, although I like her as a movie actress.

But the miserable hours of sitting in that cold theater and watching, for one of many times in my life, *Little Foxes* being chopped into a mess and misinterpreted, is not a pleasant memory.

In those days, I would leave the theater and go to lunch alone. Miss Signoret had evidently given orders to the actors to have nothing to do with me. I would take a long walk and return to the poor neighborhood where the Théâtre Sarah Bernhardt was located and find myself in a lower-class restaurant near the theater.

Now, the restaurants in this poor neighborhood are expensive. But then, they were filled with clerks and managers and salespeople and such, eating their French heads off. I don't think I knew, until those restaurants and those streets, how much Paris had changed.

Aragon died not long ago, so I guess this note of scandal can do no harm. When I first met him, he was married, or so-called married, to Elsa Triolet, a gifted woman, a novelist and the sister-in-law of Mayakovsky, the Russian poet. She was also said to have been in love with Mayakovsky himself, although it is her sister who is currently assumed to have been Mayakovsky's wife. Louis wrote a series of passionate love poems to Elsa Triolet and was, when they were together, the most loving of husbands.

When I went to the country, to the beautiful little house where the water of an old mill ran through the living room, I would sit and watch them with the greatest of envy. I was jealous, of course, of Elsa Triolet — because this handsome and enormously gifted man should love one woman so much and be so unashamed of showing it.

I don't think I've every seen love so openly displayed in writing or in the living room as Louis showed to Elsa.

Triolet died, about ten years ago, I think. I was in Paris about a year later and called Louis, as I always did when I got to Paris, but I was told he was out of town.

That night, we bumped into each other in a restaurant and had an awkward meeting. I told this to one of Louis's good friends, because I was puzzled that Louis had to lie to me about being out of town.

My friend said that wasn't the reason Louis had lied to me. He said that Louis had changed, hadn't I heard? Soon after Elsa's death, Louis had fallen in love with a boy and was now living with him.

I wouldn't believe this, until the following week, when I saw Louis in the same restaurant with a very handsome young man and this time, he got up to greet me by the door, as if to bar my way to his table. When he did go back, he kissed the young man, as if to excuse his absence.

I know no conclusion to this story, and maybe there isn't one. Aragon was always a very good writer and a fine man.

AT the end of October, 1976, Max Palevsky invited fourteen people — including me and Peter Feibleman — on a boat he chartered to go down the Nile. I didn't like all the people, but I liked most of them and it was a wonderful trip, even though my eyesight was beginning to go and I had to pass up what many of them did see.

I don't like Cairo. This was my third visit there: I made a stopover coming out of Russia, after the war, flying from Baku and then flown by the British to Teheran and then to Cairo, where the British put me up in just exactly the hotel we stayed in, on Palevsky's trip.

The hotel is near the pyramids, which I think are among the ugliest monuments ever put up by man; and I disliked the streets in 1976 as much as I disliked them during the war. The poverty is too awful.

The rich people who invited us to dinner were government people, wooing Max, and they and their houses made the contrast to the poverty even uglier. It seemed to me to sum up the situation, that out of the seven rich people, only five spoke native Egyptian. The rest had learned either Arabic or French in school and talked almost entirely in French.

The apartments or houses they lived in were rather tacky imitations of bourgeois nineteenth-century French, in architecture and furniture.

The trip down the river was wonderful. Max had put aboard some of the finest wine I've ever tasted. It drowned the difficulties the chef had with almost everything he touched, except for a large pancake, which he stuffed with anything that came from the local market. I adapted his basic recipe when I got home.

PFANNKUCHEN

Serves 2

1 1½- to 2-pound lobster
¼ cup milk
¼ cup lobster broth
2 tablespoons cornstarch
4 eggs, separated
1 teaspoon salt
¼ teaspoon white pepper
1 tablespoon parsley, minced
3 tablespoons butter

Preheat the oven to 400 degrees. Steam the lobster in 2 cups of water for 10 minutes, drain, save the broth, and pick the meat from the lobster and mince it up. Boil the broth until it reduces to ¼ cup. Add milk and dissolve the cornstarch in this mixture until it is smooth. Then set the mixture aside and let it cool. Beat the egg yolks until they are light yellow and thick. Beat the egg whites until they have stiff peaks. Fold the salt, pepper and parsley into the egg yolks, then add the milk mixture and minced lobster meat. Finally fold in the egg whites.

Melt the butter in a 10-inch skillet and swirl it around to coat the skillet. Add pancake mixture and cook over medium heat for 5 minutes. Then put the skillet in the oven until the pancake puffs up, and serve alone or with a cream sauce. I like the following creamed mussel sauce.

CREAMED MUSSEL SAUCE

Yields 1 cup

1 pound mussels, cleaned and debearded
½ cup water
¼ teaspoon lemon juice
⅛ teaspoon saffron
½ cup heavy cream
salt and pepper

Steam the mussels in ½ cup of water until they open. Drain, reserve the broth, and pick the mussels. Add the lemon juice and saffron threads to the mussel broth and simmer for 5 minutes. Add the heavy cream and simmer until thick. Add the picked mussels and some salt and pepper to taste.

Everybody who had been on the boat went their separate ways at the end of the trip, but Peter and I went to London, where Claridges Hotel must have been shocked at the amount we yelled at each other. I wanted to go to Paris and he didn't. I wanted to go to one restaurant and he didn't. I wanted to go out in the rain and he didn't. I wanted to see X friend and he didn't like X friend. I wanted to gamble and he didn't like gambling.

In any case, it turned out that he departed for Paris and I didn't. But when we stopped fighting long enough, we had one wonderful dinner with Sir Victor and Lady Pritchett, who may be among the nicest people in the world, as well as among the most distinguished. I think it was the only night when we were both too ashamed to fight, and when Peter finally admitted that he liked at least some of my friends. We went to a restaurant, Wheelers, and had a wonderful meal.

MUSHROOM BISQUE

Serves 6

1 onion, minced
2 tablespoons butter
2 pounds mushrooms, chopped
4 cups chicken broth
1 tablespoon sherry
½ cup breadcrumbs
salt and pepper

Cook the onion in butter until it is gray and soft. Add the mushrooms, chicken broth and sherry and simmer for 2 hours. Add the breadcrumbs and simmer for another ½ hour. Puree the mixture in a food processor or a blender. Return to the pan. Add salt and pepper to taste and more chicken broth if needed. Serve with a grind of black pepper.

CALF'S LIVER ON A BED OF BUTTERED APPLES

Serves 6

3 tablespoons butter
6 apples, peeled, cored and quartered
2 pounds calf's liver, sliced ⅓ inch thick
flour for dusting
salt and pepper
½ cup bacon fat
½ cup chicken broth
½ teaspoon vinegar

Melt the butter in a skillet and cook the apples until they are golden. Divide apples among 6 plates. Dust calf's liver in flour and season lightly with salt and pepper. Put the bacon fat in a skillet over high heat. Quickly fry the calf's liver, browning completely on each side. Place liver on top of buttered apples. Add stock and vinegar to pan and scrape well. Season with salt and pepper to taste and drizzle sauce over liver and apples and serve.

POTATO FRITTERS

Serves 6

2 cups grated potatoes
2 tablespoons flour
salt and pepper
1 tablespoon olive oil or bacon fat
1 egg
oil or bacon fat for frying

Mix grated potatoes with flour. Season with salt and pepper. Add olive oil. Beat in egg. Heat oil or fat and deep-fry potato mixture by teaspoonsful until all the mixture is used up. Drain the fritters on paper towels. Sprinkle with more salt and pepper and serve with liver.

POUND CAKE

One 9×5 loaf

1 cup butter
1 cup sugar
1 teaspoon bourbon
1 teaspoon grated lemon rind
4 eggs, separated
2 cups cake flour
½ teaspoon salt

Preheat oven to 325 degrees. Cream butter and sugar. Add bourbon and lemon rind and beat in egg yolks one at a time. Stir in flour and salt. Beat egg whites to stiff peaks and fold into batter. Pour batter into greased and floured 9×5-inch loaf pan and bake in 325-degree oven for one hour. Serve with fresh berries, ice cream, custard sauce or fresh fruit puree.

SIT-DOWN dinners are often only good for six to eight people. But buffet suppers are fun, and I once gave this buffet to Mike Nichols for his birthday present. Since he is a great pasta lover, he chose the kinds of pasta he wanted. It seemed to me a rather stingy dinner — but I've never seen people eat quite so much.

The recipe for Bolognese sauce was given to me, in Rome, by the mother of a chauffeur William Wyler once had. I am giving it here for twelve people. Make it for twelve and freeze what you don't use. It freezes beautifully and keeps for a long time.

BOLOGNESE SAUCE

Serves 12

¼ cup olive oil
1 pound ground beef
2 onions, minced
3 cloves garlic, minced
1 10-ounce can plum tomatoes
2 6-ounce cans tomato paste
2 cups water or meat broth
2 teaspoons salt
1 teaspoon pepper
1 teaspoon oregano
1 tablespoon basil
1 teaspoon thyme
dash of Tabasco sauce
pepperoni sausage (optional)

Put a small amount of olive oil in a large pan and sauté the meat, turning it until it browns. Add the onions and garlic, the tomatoes and the tomato paste. When you have removed the paste from the can, add 2 cups of water (or broth), scraping the remaining paste from the sides of the tin. Season the sauce with salt, pepper, oregano, basil, thyme and Tabasco. Simmer for 2½ hours. It is often very nice to add to this sauce a small amount of very finely chopped pepperoni sausage.

BASIL AND CLAM SAUCE

Serves 6

4 cloves garlic, minced
2 tablespoons olive oil
1 bunch basil, picked and minced
1 teaspoon black pepper
¼ teaspoon crushed chili pepper
20 littleneck clams, scrubbed
½ cup white wine
salt

This sauce should only be made with fresh basil. I grow it all year round in a window box. It's a hardy herb and can take a beating. Sauté the garlic in 2 tablespoons of olive oil. Add the basil, pepper and chili pepper. Add the liquor from the clams and the white wine and cook for 5 minutes. Add the clams. You must be careful not to cook the clams too much, because they toughen. Five minutes is enough. Taste the sauce for seasoning — it should have a strong garlic flavor.

SEAFOOD SAUCE

2 cloves garlic, minced
½ cup olive oil
meat from 2 lobsters, cut up fine
1 pound white fish, cut in small pieces
1 teaspoon tarragon
24 littleneck clams, scrubbed

Sauté the garlic in olive oil, add the minced lobster meat, the fish and the liquor from the clams. Cook for 5 minutes. Add the tarragon and the clams. Cook for 5 minutes and taste for seasoning.

There is a fourth sauce, although I was not able to make it the night of Nichols's birthday. It is a famous Roman sauce that is very good.

Take six ripe tomatoes, peel, seed and chop them and then cool them in the icebox. While the tomatoes are cooling, put about ½ cup of olive oil in a pan with 2 cloves of minced garlic and let it cook until barely golden. Take the pan off the heat and add the cold tomatoes. Toss with spaghetti.

I think all pasta dishes are better with very thin spaghetti, but other people like thicker spaghetti. I like imported spaghetti better than American-made spaghetti. You can buy imported Italian spaghetti at specialty shops.

When you are ready to serve your dinner, you can line all these spaghetti sauces up on a long table with Parmesan cheese or whatever cheese you like to serve with it. Nothing more is needed, except for a fruit bowl or fruit salad. It is a very good buffet supper.

13

In 1973, I went to Europe with my editor, William Abrahams, and Peter Stansky, the historian. They had been in London, but I was doing a piece for a magazine about Alsace-Lorraine and so they agreed to meet me in Strasbourg and we would go to that "charming little inn everybody knows about."

I got to Strasbourg and there was no sign of them for two hours, so I went out to the taxi line with the name of the inn and the little town in which it was located clutched in my hand. Three taxi drivers said they had never heard of it, which is quite remarkable, because Alsace-Lorraine is not a large region and the environs around Strasbourg are limited.

But one taxi driver said he did know, and off we tooted, to what turned out to be a very pleasant, run-down castle, which a Baron something-or-other owned. I went to bed immediately and was awakened by the tooting of Billy's car.

He had been overanxious that I had got lost in Strasbourg. So overanxious that he didn't bother to explain to me that his plane had been late leaving London, the reason for the lost hours.

I don't think I thought the charming castle quite as charming as Billy did, but in any case, we ate superbly.

A few days later, we drove across France to another little inn near Avallon. This one was truly charming, though the food was not. After dinner on the second night, I, who have seldom been sick in my whole life, did a very remarkable thing, although I have little memory of it.

Billy says they came to find me in the morning and I wouldn't answer my door, which had been carefully locked, so they had somebody climb in the window. I was stretched on the bed with a cut on my forehead; the heavy bedside table had been overturned. He insisted that I get a doctor, I insisted that I didn't want a doctor and so I stayed up all day, pretending that I felt all right, not knowing what was the matter with me and irritated that anything was. The next day I felt worse, and Billy called the doctor. When the doctor came he tickled my feet with a safety pin and said he thought I'd better go to a hospital. I said I didn't want to go to a local hospital, and so a younger doctor was brought in. He did some more tests, whatever they were, and finally concluded that I should go to the American hospital in Paris, by ambulance. I think it was the longest ride of my life — semiconscious, not knowing what had happened to me and being, most of the time, unable to communicate with the drivers, who talked the Alsace-Lorraine French-German that I once knew (because I grew up with it) but had long ago lost and was too sick to remember.

I landed in the American hospital in Paris, to see my old friends, Gold and Fizdale, the pianists, sitting in the room waiting for me. I still do not know how they knew I was arriving, except that Billy probably called them before he and Stansky drove to Paris.

I don't remember the next two or three days very well, except that a good many tests were done on me. I was in a room with a very nice lady, who gave me a large bottle of perfume for a present when she got up to leave. On my fifth day in the hospital, I began to grow very nervous about the hospital itself, and on the sixth day, I decided to leave.

I packed my bag and carried it downstairs, waiting for somebody to stop me. Nobody did. I went by taxi to Air France and from Air France back to New York. Nothing more was ever discovered about this incident, no cause, I mean, although Robert Lowell, who had heard about it and offered to help, thought it was a stroke. Peter, who thought the same thing, met me at Kennedy Airport and was all for transporting me immediately to another hospital. I was all for not going, so we had a royal battle in the airport. (Peter is convinced that any action he does is a piece of giant nobility and entitles him to boss you around, forever.)

I didn't go to another hospital and I have no idea to this day what caused the episode, although it may have been the beginnings of all that has happened since. But no doctor seems to be interested in it, so it's very possible that Mr. Peter Feibleman is the best doctor of all.

Anyway, in the American hospital in Paris, whose food is almost as bad as any other hospital, the very nice Mme. Houbigant of the Houbigant perfumes took pity on me and had her cook make me a wonderful small broiled chicken. I do not think we have these chickens any longer in America, although I grew up on them, but in case you can find them or in case you raise them, this is the recipe.

SMALL BROILED CHICKEN

Allowing one broiler per person, take each broiler, not much larger than a squab, about 1¼ pounds, and dust with tarragon, salt, pepper and melted butter.

Put it under a decent flame to brown, then turn the flame down. Cook for no more than 20 minutes, adding a little tarragon and a jigger of white wine to it.

At the very end, pour over it a little cream that has been warmed on the stove with a little vodka. If it is necesasary to crisp it again, turn up the flame. It's a wonderful dish, particularly for someone who is ill.

14

THE big occasion before Lent in New Orleans, of course, is Mardi Gras. I suppose I grew tired of Mardi Gras as a small child. I was yanked back and forth to the houses of people who lived on St. Charles Avenue and propped up on something large enough to hold me, so that I could see over the heads of grown-ups.

I was always uncomfortable. I never liked the whole parade and I never liked running out into the street, which I was urged to do, to collect things thrown from floats. Early on, it seemed to me a form of begging, and thus demeaning.

When I was about twelve, I put my foot down very firmly against ever seeing Carnival again, but eight or ten years ago, Peter and I found ourselves in New Orleans after Mardi Gras was over. I had flown down to see my two wonderful spinster aunts, who lived as happy women, in a modest half-house, loving each other and the world.

My one aunt was a very great cook. She asked me, of course, to have Easter dinner and to bring somebody if I wanted to. I brought Peter, and this is the fine dinner she cooked.

CLAMS À LA OREGANO

Serves 4

24 littleneck clams on the halfshell
1 tablespoon organo
4–5 slices bacon cut into ¼-inch pieces

Preheat broiler. Put a very small touch of oregano on each clam and top with a tiny piece of bacon. Run the clams under the broiler for a few minutes. The bacon should sizzle a little bit, but not really fry. Remove the clams carefully, since the shells will be hot. I find it pleasant to fry an extra 4 or 5 slices of bacon until they are crisp. Crunch them up and put a little bit of this crunchy bacon on each clam before serving.

ROAST CAPON WITH NEW POTATOES

Serves 4

1 capon
salt and pepper
1 onion, quartered
1 clove garlic, peeled
2 tablespoons butter, softened
1 tablespoon rosemary
12 new potatoes in their jackets
1 cup white wine

Preheat the oven to 350 degrees. Salt and pepper the bird inside and out. Place the onion and garlic in the cavity. Rub the skin with butter and sprinkle with rosemary. Truss the capon. Place in oven and roast for about one hour. Add the potatoes and turn the oven up to 450 degrees for about 30 to 45 more minutes and baste the bird and the potatoes with the butter and fat from the bottom of the pan. When the capon is done, remove the bird and the potatoes. Put the roasting pan on the top of the stove and add the white wine. Scrape the pan very well over a medium flame. Carve the bird and drizzle the pan sauce over each serving.

ITALIAN-STYLE SPINACH

Serves 4

1 onion, minced
2 cloves garlic, minced
2 tablespoons olive oil
1 pound spinach, washed and chopped fine
2 tablespoons Parmesan cheese, grated

Sauté the onion and garlic in olive oil until soft. Add the spinach and toss to warm. Keep turning the spinach over so that it is thoroughly mixed with the oil and garlic. Sprinkle a little Parmesan cheese over the top. That is all.

Make a fine salad and by fine, I mean fine. There seems to be a great mystery about making salads and salad dressing and there is no mystery.

The so-called mystery can be solved by buying good olive oil and good vinegar. Those who make poor dressing buy neither. Exact measurements cannot be given — if your vinegar is old, which it should be, you will need less vinegar and more oil. If it is fresh wine vinegar, you will use less. You can add any herb you like, or no herb at all. You can, if you like, add a peeled piece of garlic and let it rest in the dressing for an hour or two. But please take it out before serving the salad. I think that after an hour or two, garlic gets slightly bitter and rancid.

The proportions are about right. If you need more dressing, just increase the ingredients in the same proportion:

BASIC FRENCH DRESSING
or Vinaigrette

1 teaspoon salt
½ teaspoon black pepper
½ teaspoon mustard (I like Dijon mustard but use your own favorite)
¼ cup white wine vinegar
1 cup olive oil

Place salt, pepper, mustard and vinegar in a stainless steel bowl. Whisk to combine. Continue whisking while adding oil in a slow, steady stream.

If you like, you can end this dinner with a salad and a variety of cheese. But my aunt didn't. And I agree with her — a dessert is in order.

PEACH COBBLER

THE PASTRY:

2 cups all-purpose flour
2 teaspoons baking powder
½ teaspoon salt
2 tablespoons sugar
5 tablespoons melted butter
2 eggs
½ cup milk

Combine the dry ingredients. Make a well in the center. Combine butter, eggs and milk, pour into the well, and stir with flour mixture. Turn dough onto a lightly floured surface and knead briefly until all ingredients are well combined.

THE FILLING:

4 cups peeled and sliced peaches
½ cup sugar
1 teaspoon lemon juice
1 tablespoon all-purpose flour
2 tablespoons bourbon

Toss all filling ingredients in a bowl.

TO ASSEMBLE:

Grease a cake pan with butter and fill the pan with the fruit mixture. Dot the mixture with butter. Being a sticky dough, the cobbler pastry is difficult to roll. It is easiest to pull small pieces of the dough and flatten by hand to cover the peach mixture. When the mixture is covered with a thick layer of dough, bake the cobbler at 350 degrees for 45 minutes or until the crust is golden.

On this visit, I stayed with my aunts. They liked Peter, as they liked almost everybody, and he liked them, because they had charming, funny stories about their life in New Orleans and themselves or me as a child or their father or my father.

The next day, my aunt asked me back, because she said she

had a Virginia ham. She had been preparing this ham for many days before I got there.

There is, to my mind, no delicacy finer than a well-cooked and well-smoked Virginia ham, but they are not easy to find. The ones called Smithfield, which are sold in stores, are not highly enough smoked. Virginia ham is salty and tough and, I think, wonderful. But it must be sliced paper thin or else it cannot be eaten and it must be cooked to perfection. I think it is one of the great American dishes and has been totally ruined by the common variety of ham, lowering the American standards of cooking and taste.

You must send away to a place in either Kentucky or Virginia to get the real thing, but you have to like Virginia-cured ham. There are also a number of places that sell highly spiced Virginia ham, but they are usually more expensive.

Here are two addresses. There are many more.

S. Wallace Edwards & Sons
Surry, Virginia 23883

R. L. Christian & Co., Inc.
204 North Robinson Street
Richmond, Virginia 23220

I always keep one in my icebox. You do not have to worry about it. It can remain there for a year.

William Styron, the novelist, doesn't bother with an icebox. He keeps his hung in his cellar. If you have a cellar, you would do equally well to keep one there. That was the way our forefathers kept them.

If it's easier to handle, and it frequently is, ask your butcher to cut off about 4 or 5 inches of the small end of the ham for you. Save that ham butt for other occasions, such as cooking beans or soup or anything that needs it. It is very precious.

When you get ready to use it, scrub it very well with a fine steel brush. Pay no attention to the white spots on the skin, which you might mistake for mildew. They are not. The white spots are just accumulations of salt.

Soak the ham anywhere from 12 to 24 hours in cold water, changing the water once. Then, using the same large kettle in which you have soaked it, bring the water to a boil and reduce the flame to a simmer.

I really mean simmer. It must barely bubble. Cover the top and allow anything from 6 to 8 hours. The time will vary, of course, depending on the weight of the ham and often upon the stove.

The ham is done only when the small bone at the end begins to come loose from the flesh. Let it cool enough to be handled, but that is all. Do not let it stay in the hot water for too long.

Take it out of the water and put it someplace where you can handle it easily. With a sharp knife, remove the top skin, which will come off very easily, leaving a large layer of fat.

Cut away the fat, leaving only about ½ to ¾ inch over the top. Please do not cut any further than that. A ham should have fat on it in order to keep properly and, because it is so big, you will probably not be able to use more than half of it in one meal.

Now comes the problem. I had a great cook who absolutely refused to bake the ham. She was, in many ways, right. The ham is really now finished. But many people believe in a 20-minute baking period, and so I am giving it here.

Stick 12 to 14 cloves in the fat of the ham. Be careful not to use too many cloves. The flavor of this ham should not have as much clovey taste as usual. Preheat the oven to 350 degrees. Take 1 tablespoon brown sugar and scatter it over the top of the fat. Take 2 jiggers of bourbon and throw over ham.

Bake 20 to 25 minutes, basting it twice during that period.

This ham must be, *must be* sliced very, very thin. It is inedible if you don't. Its best nature is that it's tough. Carving is the only difficult part. You need a very sharp, long, thin knife. Start by making the incision toward the bone end and slice away three or four slices, which you will use for some other purpose, some other day, until you are now getting to the real meat of the ham.

Cut it on the bias, very thinly. If you don't have the confidence of a good carver, do not buy this ham, because it is a waste of money and will be too tough to eat.

The ham is traditionally served in the South with black-eyed peas. Here is a recipe for black-eyed peas.

BLACK-EYED PEAS

Put one package of black-eyed peas in a colander or strainer and wash very well. Put them on to boil with 1 cut-up onion, 1 cut-up piece of garlic, 1 crushed bay leaf and a little thyme. Simmer until done. You may also add a pinch of oregano to the peas if you like. Oregano is very pleasant.

For dessert, you might try this recipe for chocolate pecan pie.

CHOCOLATE PECAN PIE

PASTRY:

2 sticks sweet butter, chilled
2 cups flour
2 teaspoons salt
1 egg yolk
3 tablespoons cold water

Cut the cold butter into small chunks. Combine flour and salt. On work surface, cover butter with flour and salt. Combine with fingertips until the mixture is like coarse cornmeal. Combine egg yolk and water. Form a well in the flour mixture. Pour in egg yolk and water and quickly work dough with the heel of your hand to a smooth consistency. Chill.

PIE FILLING:

5 eggs
2 tablespoons bourbon
½ cup brown sugar
½ cup light corn syrup
1 teaspoon salt
1 tablespoon flour
4 cups pecans
½ cup semisweet chocolate bits

Beat together eggs, bourbon, brown sugar, corn syrup, salt and flour. Fold in pecans.

TO ASSEMBLE PIE:

Roll out crust and lay in pie plate. Cover the bottom with semisweet chocolate bits and pour in filling. Bake at 350 degrees until crust is golden and filling is fairly solid to touch — about 45 minutes, but check the pie after 30 minutes.

15

SEVERAL years ago I went down to see Peter Feibleman when he was finishing a novel in New Orleans. We began to have an argument almost immediately, because Peter likes crummy hotels and I do not.

He was living in the Quarter, which all New Orleans and most New Yorkers love but I do not love. Perhaps because when I was a child my aunt used to take me down to bookstores in the Quarter and allow me to buy secondhand books there or anything else that took my fancy. I loved the trips and I loved the books, but I never liked the Quarter after I saw two rats jump down from a bookshelf. (Ever since then I have been rat crazy.) After that I would never allow anybody to take me to the Quarter again.

Peter's hotel, it seemed to me, was located just where I had seen the rats, which of course was nonsense, since I don't remember where I saw them. But every time I went to visit him to talk about the novel, I was sure there was a rat about to come out of the wall.

In any case, after a week's visit, I said that I would no longer stay downstairs in his hotel, but would move myself somewhere else unless he promised to move. And so we both moved: I to the nice clean Pontchartrain Hotel and he to an apartment with a beautiful courtyard on Bourbon Street. It is perfectly true that there couldn't be a rowdier street in the world than Bourbon

Street, but once inside the courtyard the beautiful trees and flowers, for me, wiped out all such considerations, and the apartment was charming.

I fixed Peter's first meal in the apartment. I was trying to teach him to save money, which was a totally unsuccessful venture, and so I never tried again. But this is a rather good meal I did fix.

New Orleans is famous for a dish called Red Beans and Rice. Both he and I had grown up on it. When I was a child, it was always Monday's dish because you used the leftover ham from Sunday's meal.

RED BEANS AND RICE

1 ham hock
1 package red beans
1 onion, minced
2 cloves garlic, minced
2 bay leaves
½ teaspoon oregano
½ teaspoon basil
¼ teaspoon crushed red chili pepper
dash of Worcestershire sauce

Wash the beans. Do not soak them, no matter what it says on the package. Put the beans in a large pot with the ham hock and enough cold water to cover. Add the onion, garlic, bay leaves, oregano, basil and chili pepper. Add a dash of Worcestershire sauce. Start the mixture to boiling. When it reaches a boil, reduce it to a simmer and keep tasting to see if your beans are done. When the beans are soft enough, turn them off. I like using half of the beans to make soup with and half of them to eat with rice.

Take half of the beans and all of the water and put it through a food processor along with any pieces of ham that you can pull off the ham hock. This will mash it all up for soup. Leave the other half of the beans whole and serve with white rice. In New Orleans this dish is often served with a minced purple onion on top.

16

I HAVE no idea whether a "*Dinner in Remembrance of*" was a custom only in my family. Perhaps they invented it, since I have never heard of its being done anyplace else. In order to put it down here, I have questioned a number of people and have come up with nobody else who grew up with such a custom. But in my family it was done, particularly by my father and by his two sisters. I think they considered themselves exemplary characters for doing it. The way other people possibly went to church on an anniversary of a death, they instead ate a good dinner and made some speeches and lifted their glasses. It seems to me a nice custom, and so I am giving the kind of dinner they used to have and even a taste of the speech my father used to make.

They always had a dinner, for example, on the anniversary of their father's death. My aunts and my father had always spoken of my grandfather as a Civil War hero. He had come to this country not long before the Civil War, did have a number of real decorations, but they never seemed to be able to answer the question of what he had gotten them for, because they didn't seem clear about where he had been stationed.

At eighteen, thinking I was bright and really with nothing more in my head than the desire to give my aunts and my father more knowledge than they seemed to have, I did some research work in the library. Yes, my grandfather had come just in time for the Civil War, had earned three medals, but now I knew the answer to what they evidently never knew: where he had been stationed and what battles he had fought. So I happily went home to this eighteenth dinner celebration to tell them what I thought was a comic tale: God knows how he had earned the medals. He fought in no battles because he had been quartermaster general stationed in Florida to check the food supplies coming through. I had lifted my glass in honor of the appreciation speech, but the minute I spoke my news my father knocked the glass from my hand and my one aunt began to cry very hard. My father said, "Wherever he is sitting in heaven, let us hope your grandfather forgives you." I went flying across the street to a friendly neighbor's to explain the trouble I was in and to cry my eyes out for the rest of the night. My mistake was never mentioned again, and as far as I know my grandfather went back to being a hero.

They had honored my grandfather by having the dinner that he evidently liked best: it was boiled short ribs and a soup from the short ribs. But somewhere the custom had been broken, because they never again had a party in honor of my grandfather or if they did they didn't invite me.

My father would never stand to speak. He would simply raise his champagne glass and say, "My beloved ones [or "my dearly beloved ones"], we have chosen this meal to honor our dead. I would like all of you to enjoy yourselves and at the end of it rise in a salute to our parents. Thank you. Now begin."

We began with short ribs.

BOILED SHORT RIBS

Serves 6

6 short ribs
2 pounds beef chuck
1 10-ounce can Italian tomatoes
1 onion, minced
1 clove garlic, minced
2 bay leaves
1 tablespoon salt
1 tablespoon pepper
1 teaspoon basil

½ teaspoon oregano
1 teaspoon thyme
1 tablespoon parsley
dash of Tabasco sauce
dash of Worcestershire sauce
1 rutabaga, peeled and quartered
5 carrots, peeled and cut in half
5 parsnips, peeled and cut in half
1 teaspoon vinegar

Cover the meat to twice its depth with water in a tall pot. Add tomatoes, onion, garlic, bay leaves, salt, pepper, basil, oregano, thyme, parsley, Tabasco sauce and Worcestershire sauce. Bring to a boil, turn to simmer, and cover the pot. Add the rutabaga. Simmer for 3 hours and taste. You will probably need a little more salt and pepper. Add carrots and parsnips and cook one more hour.

Test the short ribs for softness. If they are soft, take them out and put in a separate pan to keep warm. Turn the soup back on and let the chuck cook for another 15 minutes. This is an excellent soup and these are the ways to serve it.

Have it for that night's dinner or save the soup and have the short ribs for dinner with a strong horseradish sauce (recipe follows). On the following day, take out the chuck and cut it into small pieces and make a nice meat salad. Or serve the whole thing as a one-pot dinner with Parmesan cheese sprinkled on top.

Have a green salad with some good ripe cheese. End the meal with a nice hot apple tart.

SOUR CREAM AND HORSERADISH SAUCE

Yields 1 cup

1 teaspoon mustard, Dijon style
3 tablespoons fresh grated horseradish
1 cup sour cream
1 teaspoon salt
½ teaspoon pepper

Combine all ingredients and allow to steep in refrigerator overnight. Add additional horseradish to taste for additional sharpness.

TARTE TATIN

1 recipe of basic pastry (see recipe page 62)
¼ cup sweet butter
¾ cup 10X sugar (confectioner's)
¼ cup water
1 pound tart apples, peeled, seeded and cut into quarters

Preheat the oven to 350 degrees. Place butter, sugar and water in a skillet and cook over medium heat until the sugar begins to caramelize. When the mixture is slightly golden, remove from heat. Place apples in the skillet and shake the skillet to allow caramelized sugar to coat the first layer of apples. Roll out the pie dough and cover apples, tucking the pastry over the apples to form a thick edge around the skillet. Place skillet in 350-degree oven for 40 minutes or until the pastry is crisp and golden. Remove from oven. Place a large round plate over the skillet, turn out the tart like an upside-down cake, and serve warm with whipped cream or alone.

17

ONCE upon a time, according to the *Oxford English Dictionary*, St. Valentine's Day was set up to commemorate two Italian saints, Valentin and Valentinus. We suppose they were lovers, although saints are not supposed to be lovers, so maybe they were a nice old married couple who became saints because somebody wanted them to be saints, a long time later.

Great festivals were held in his, her or their honor. We wouldn't think you would now want a great festival dinner, because somewhere around 1825 the whole thing was cut down to the exchange of cards or pieces of paper with things drawn on them; sometimes with genuine messages of love and sometimes with comic messages of love. Our time, I think, has brought a pleasant compromise in certain parts of the South. You send somebody you love, or like very much, some flowers or an unsigned card and let them guess who likes them so much. Then you fess up and ask them over for dinner.

Stretch out the money and buy a couple of bottles of very good wine, both red and white. Have enough stuff on the bar to have a couple of drinks before supper.

I like serving the following dishes to special people on St. Valentine's Day. For dessert, I make or buy a simple cake with Valentine icing.

BEET AND ENDIVE AND WALNUT SALAD

Serves 6

3 endives, cut into ½-inch slices
3 beets, peeled, cooked and sliced thin
½ cup toasted walnuts
½ cup walnut vinaigrette (recipe follows)

Toss endives, beets and walnuts gently with vinaigrette sauce and serve.

Walnut Oil Vinaigrette

1 shallot, minced
3 tablespoons champagne vinegar
1 cup walnut oil
salt and pepper

Combine shallot and vinegar and slowly whisk in walnut oil. Season with salt and pepper to taste.

RABBIT OR HARE

Serves 6

1½ pounds pork belly, chopped
3 carrots, peeled and chopped
1½ onions, minced
1 clove garlic, minced
1 teaspoon thyme
1 bay leaf
1 rabbit, cut up
1 cup dry white wine
¼ cup brandy
1 egg yolk
2 tablespoons heavy cream
1 teaspoon Dijon mustard
1 teaspoon chopped parsley
salt and pepper

Lay ½ pound of the pork in the bottom of a casserole. Cover with a layer of half the carrot, onion, garlic, thyme, bay leaf, and add another ½ pound of the pork. Add the rabbit, then the rest of the vegetables and the rest of the pork. Pour the wine and brandy over the casserole. Cover tightly and cook in a slow oven (about 300 degrees) for 2½ hours. Remove, arrange meat and vegetables on serving dish and keep warm. Skim the fat off the cooking juices and place casserole on low flame. Beat the egg yolk and cream together and add to the juices, stir, and cook gently. DO NOT BOIL, just cook until it thickens, add the mustard, and pour over the rabbit. Sprinkle with parsley.

GARLIC AND PARMESAN POTATOES

Serves 6

6 Idaho potatoes, sliced thin
2 cloves garlic, minced
2 tablespoons butter
fresh minced chives (optional)
2 tablespoons grated Parmesan cheese

Preheat the oven to 350 degrees. Put the potatoes in a baking pan, letting each slice barely touch the other slices and arranging in a ring. Sprinkle the garlic over the potatoes. Dot the potatoes with butter and perhaps a sprinkling of fresh minced chives. Sprinkle with Parmesan cheese and put the potatoes in the 350-degree oven to cook for 30 to 35 minutes until mildly brown.

18

I HAVE a nice memory of St. Patrick's Day, 1965. Peter and I were put down in County Clare in the days when BOAC and almost all American planes refueled in Shannon. I think we both got very drunk at the airport and we began to wander around the town. I, for a very long time, used to have arguments with Dashiell Hammett about the Irish. He claimed I was a sucker for the Irish, and should have been born one. I claimed I would like to have been born one, and when I said that, he would turn his face away in horror. This time I thought if I could persuade Peter to rent a car, I would see something of the land.

I cannot any longer remember what directions we took, since the driver of the car was Peter, who, wherever he drives, even in his own driveway, thinks he is lost. But Ireland of course is not an easy place to find your way around in. We had set out to find Elizabeth Bowen in the hope that she would put us up for a day, but we soon gave up that plan. The drive through Limerick was through very beautiful land, the kind of land I like best in the world: fine farmland with low stone walls built not to keep man out but to keep beast in. Along the coast road, from Limerick to Kerry, which Peter I think had chosen by mistake, the dunes, unlike most dunes, were not depressing. We stopped along the way, and tried taking our clothes off on a rock and jumping into the ocean from there. Peter made it but I didn't, because I lost my nerve.

There was a long drop but I climbed down and made it to a lower level and fell off into the water. It was one of the loveliest swims I ever had, because the formation of the land made twists and turns, thus it was impossible for the ocean to stay in any one angry spot. Instead, it left behind small coves of water and rocks. After a very long time Peter pressed me to come out of the water, and I dried on the rocks in the sun. Because we were both happy, we took each other by the hand and walked off across the dunes into the small and charming village. It was a fortunate day.

I had once had a trained nurse whose husband came from the village. As soon as I made this known to the man who brought our beers, it seemed to me that people came from every direction to ask questions about their son, or cousin, or friend. We asked where to stay and were politely conducted by half the village to a simple house along the main street, where we had two clean rooms with wonderful beds and feather quilts I have never forgotten. The next morning was cold and getting dressed was not pleasant, but when we went downstairs to an enormous breakfast we weren't cold anymore, because the huge fireplace could heat the entire house.

They were fine people living on this beautiful land. Half of them farmed for a living and half of them fished. We were taken down to see the boats, which are made by the natives and of interesting design. They are made of ash and in the old days were tied together with leather thongs. But of course now they are nailed, though a few were still tied together with thongs and the workmanship was beautiful. They were big, heavy, sturdy boats and the people told me the story of a man whose name I cannot remember who had left this beach one August morning without saying anything and turned up on a Caribbean island a year and a half later.

I have long known that I am very romantic about boats and about fishermen who go out in them by themselves, because all my life I have fished and all my life have been tempted to do nothing else. Later in the day, when the man who had made the voyage by himself came to visit the house we were in, and Peter said, introducing him, "This is Lillian Hellman who is already in love with you, sir," he said, "That's very nice," in a calm voice and sat down to take his tea. His wife shouted at him that I was a stranger and was in love with him. He took it all very calmly and said that was his good luck perhaps because it was St. Patrick's Day and what were they having for dinner? I foolishly said, "I am sure corned beef and cabbage." The wonderful-looking captain said, "And I am sure not. We never have corned beef and cabbage. It's your American idea of what the Irish eat. We will have a piece of boiled bacon which we cured last year and some potatoes which we dug from the soil and a cabbage which is ready for us now. It has been put aside in the root cellar." And that is just what we did have.

BACON AND CABBAGE

Serves 4

1 pound bacon
1 cabbage, quartered
1 tablespoon mustard
2 tablespoons brown sugar
1 cup breadcrumbs
½ ounce bourbon

Boil the bacon for one hour. Remove, cool, and set aside. Add the cabbage to the bacon broth and simmer. In the meantime remove the rind from the bacon. Coat the bacon with mustard, brown sugar and breadcrumbs. Then sprinkle the bourbon over it and broil until the bacon becomes golden brown and crisp.

Slice the bacon thin, and serve each person a piece of cabbage, some bacon and perhaps some small boiled potatoes.

You should obviously have a simple dessert with this excellent dish. Perhaps cut-up fruit is best, although the Irish frequently have rhubarb pie. But I am not a rhubarb girl so I cannot recommend it. I recommend an apple baked in cider — remember to serve your bacon and cabbage with plenty of Guinness Stout or beer.

APPLES BAKED IN CIDER

¼ cup brown sugar
½ teaspoon cinnamon
6 tart apples, washed and cored
½ cup butter
1 cup apple cider

Combine brown sugar and cinnamon. Fill cored apples with mixture and place apples in baking dish. Slice a pat of butter onto each apple. Bring cider to a boil, pour around apples, and bake at 350 degrees for 30 minutes.

My most memorable St. Patrick's Day in America was quite different. Dorothy Parker and I had decided to drive to my house in Martha's Vineyard and we forgot that it was St. Patrick's Day. Parker was half Irish and half Jewish, and sometimes she was very anti-Irish and sometimes very anti-Jewish. Today, on this day of hard driving and rerouting, she was very anti-Irish. The number of epithets to come out of her mouth was amazing in variety and sometimes in length. Driving does not go with laughing too much, and the more I laughed, the more remarkable grew her anger with the Irish. By the time we got to the traffic on Major Deegan Parkway, they were even responsible for Hitler's Holocaust.

When we finally did get to the Vineyard, I said that I thought we should have a St. Patrick's Day supper. She said that she wouldn't have a St. Patrick's Day supper. She said she wouldn't eat a bite in the name of St. Patrick.

I said, "Let's change the name to St. Justin."

"Who in hell is St. Justin?" she said.

I can't remember who I made St. Justin, but in any case we had this very good meal.

ROAST DUCK

Serves 2 to 4

1 fresh duck
1 onion
1 clove garlic
1 inch fresh ginger root
¼ cup soy sauce
1 tablespoon sesame oil

Cut away the tail and all possible fat off the duck. Rub the duck inside and out with salt and pepper. Put the onion, garlic and ginger inside the duck and truss it up. Combine the soy sauce and sesame oil and brush the skin of the duck. Roast the duck in a 350-degree oven for about 2½ hours. The duck will grow crisp and fine.

I do not believe that duck needs any kind of jelly, but it does need a tart salad — green or wax beans in a vinaigrette is nice. And please, violate all today's rules and leave off oranges from the duck. In spite of the French, I think they are a bad combination. Crepes are a fine addition to this dinner (I use the crepes to roll around bits of duck). And so is pineapple lemon ice (recipe page 36).

GREEN OR WAX BEANS IN A WARM VINAIGRETTE

1 pound green or wax beans, snapped
4 strips bacon
2 tablespoons sherry vinegar
olive oil
fresh rosemary
salt and pepper
1 clove garlic, minced

Blanch the beans. Drain and cool completely under cold water. Fry bacon until crisp, then remove bacon and reserve. Over high heat add garlic to bacon grease and deglaze the pan with sherry vinegar, scraping with a wooden spoon. Add rosemary and remove from heat. Add olive oil (up to 1 cup) and whisk to emulsify. Season with salt and pepper. Toss beans in warm vinaigrette and serve garnished with bacon strips at room temperature.

CREPES

1 cup flour
⅓ teaspoon salt
1 cup milk
3 eggs
2 tablespoons melted butter
additional butter for frying

Combine flour and salt in a bowl. Make a well in the center. Combine eggs, milk and melted butter and pour into the well of flour. Combine ingredients with as few strokes as possible (overbeating will make a tough crepe), and pass batter through a fine mesh strainer to remove lumps. Allow to rest in refrigerator before frying. Add additional milk to thin if necessary.

19

FOR a weekend in the country, when you don't feel like spending your life in the kitchen and when you wish to take enough food from the city to last the whole weekend, try packing: two cold roasted chickens (recipe page 27), French bread, some ground chuck, ground sirloin, some cabbage, lettuce, onions, vinegar and oil, eggs, potatoes, a well-aged Brie and some fresh fruit, and make yourself a chocolate cake that will last the whole weekend. And try these recipes:

HAMBURGERS

Serves 6

2 pounds ground sirloin
1 pound ground chuck
1 onion, minced
1 clove garlic, minced
½ teaspoon olive oil
dash of Worcestershire sauce
1 teaspoon catsup
½ teaspoon salt
¼ teaspoon pepper
½ cup parsley, minced

Put all the ingredients in a big bowl and mix it thoroughly with your hands. Pat into 8-ounce patties and grill. You will have to ask each person how they like the hamburgers. For very rare it will take no more than 2 minutes to a side; for medium it should take 3 or 4 minutes on each side; for those villains who eat it well done, it can cook for 7 or 8 minutes on each side.

COLE SLAW

1 teaspoon vinegar
1 teaspoon lemon juice
½ teaspoon salt
¼ teaspoon pepper
dash of Tabasco sauce
dash of Worcestershire sauce
½ teaspoon celery seeds
1 tablespoon fresh dill
1 cup mayonnaise
2 cups shredded cabbage
2 cups shredded red cabbage

Place vinegar, lemon juice, salt, pepper, Tabasco sauce, Worcestershire sauce, celery seeds and dill in a mixing bowl. Combine well and whisk in the mayonnaise. Check the seasoning, and adjust with more salt and pepper or additional dill or celery seed if desired. Add the shredded cabbage and red cabbage. Toss to coat completely. Chill for one hour before serving.

RED POTATO SALAD

8 cups red potatoes, cut in quarters
1 teaspoon salt
½ teaspoon black pepper
1 teaspoon mustard
⅛ cup lemon juice
⅛ cup white wine vinegar
1 cup olive oil
½ cup chopped parsley

Place quartered potatoes in a large pot of cold water. Cook over high heat until the potatoes are beginning to soften. While potatoes are cooking, place salt, pepper, mustard, lemon juice and vinegar in a large bowl and whisk to combine. Continue whisking while adding olive oil in a slow, steady stream. When potatoes are tender, drain into a colander. Toss warm potatoes in dressing along with chopped parsley. Add additional salt and pepper if desired and chill until ready to serve.

MISSISSIPPI MUD CAKE

½ cup bourbon
1½ cups coffee
5 ounces unsweetened chocolate
2 cups sugar
pinch of salt
2 cups all-purpose flour
1 teaspoon baking soda
¾ teaspoon baking powder
5 eggs
2 tablespoons vanilla

Preheat the oven to 275 degrees. Melt the chocolate in the bourbon and coffee. Add sugar and salt. Combine flour, baking soda and powder and gradually beat into the chocolate mixture. Do not overbeat. Lightly mix eggs and vanilla into the batter. Pour into a buttered and floured tube pan and bake at 275 degrees for about 1½ hours. The cake is done when a toothpick inserted in the center comes out clean.

20

WHEN I told Hannah Weinstein about this book, she asked if I would be including any recipes for Jewish dishes. I said yes, if she would supply them. The very next day a batch arrived from her. That was characteristic of Hannah: generous, prompt, and true to her word.

I'm sorry to have to add to this that Hannah died, suddenly and unexpectedly, only a few months ago. It pleases me that the final words of my portion of this book should be hers.

LATKES

6 potatoes
1 small onion
3 tablespoons flour
1 teaspoon salt
¼ teaspoon pepper
¼ teaspoon baking powder
2 eggs, lightly beaten

Peel and grate the potatoes and onion and squeeze in a towel to dry. Stir in flour, salt, pepper, baking powder and eggs. Drop by spoonfuls into a hot, well-greased skillet. Serve with hot apple sauce, sugar or sour cream.

APPLE SAUCE

1 pound tart apples
½ cup sugar
½ teaspoon vanilla

½ cup water
juice of ½ lemon plus zest of ½ lemon

Place all ingredients in pot and cook, covered, over low heat until apples are soft. Stir to puree texture and serve warm.

POT ROAST

Serves 6

1 brisket of beef
flour
salt and pepper
2 tablespoons rendered suet
1 onion, chopped fine
2 carrots, peeled and chopped
2 stalks celery, chopped
1 bay leaf
3 cups meat stock (chicken or beef broth)

Cut off the thicker end of a brisket of beef and use only the thin end in this recipe. You can freeze the thick end for soup or stew. Dust the thin end with flour and season with salt and pepper. Brown it well in rendered suet. Add the onion, carrots, celery and bay leaf. Pour in the meat broth and cook for 2 hours until tender. Taste the broth and add salt and pepper if necessary.

HAMANTASCHEN

4 cups flour
3 teaspoons baking powder
¾ cup sugar
¼ teaspoon salt
4 eggs
⅓ cup vegetable oil
minced rind of 1 lemon
prune filling (recipe follows)

Mix all the dry ingedients. In a separate bowl combine eggs, oil and lemon rind. With a few quick strokes add the dry ingredients to the egg mixture and knead this mixture until satiny. Roll out on a floured board to ⅛-inch thickness. Cut in 4-inch rounds. Place a heaping teaspoon of filling in the center of each and bring the edges together to form a triangle. Pinch the edges together to close securely. Bake on a greased cookie sheet in a 375-degree oven until browned. It usually takes 30 minutes.

PRUNE FILLING

1 pound prunes
2 teaspoons lemon juice
rind of 1 lemon

Soak the prunes in water, brandy or wine until soft. Then warm gently in the same liquid over medium heat for about 15 minutes. Remove the pits and chop the prunes very fine. Add the lemon juice and lemon rind.

HIS WAY

Peter Feibleman

Martha's Vineyard

MOST only children in New Orleans grow up in the kitchen, and I was used to watching a bay leaf dropped into a pot long before I was tall enough to know what the pot contained. I much preferred sitting in the kitchen to sitting in the living room, but once in a while I had no choice: I first met Lillian Hellman early one evening when I was told by my parents to come downstairs in my pajamas and robe and say hello to the dinner guests. I already had a jaundiced eye. Faulkner, Henry Miller, Sherwood Anderson had all been around, and my father was himself a writer. I remember being told that Lillian's first play, *The Children's Hour*, was a big success in New York, but that didn't mean a whole lot. What meant a whole lot was the look of her back when I was walking downstairs. I had never seen anybody stand like that. Lillian was the only person I had met who didn't talk down to children. She asked me how old I was and when I told her I was "only ten," she nodded and her face didn't change. "I don't know what you mean by 'only.' Ten isn't so young," she said and turned away.

I wasn't at all sure what she meant by the remark but I remember thinking she was nobody to argue with.

As of September, 1983, she still isn't, and one of the subjects she likes to argue about is cooking. Food is taken very seriously in South Louisiana; I once knew two families who stopped speaking for seven years because of an argument about whether okra or filé powder should be used as a thickener in gumbo. New Orleans people are the worst food-fighters of all: I was ten when I met Lillian, eighteen when we disagreed about a shrimp dish and twenty-eight when we argued for a week about how to make chicken soup.

We are, in fact, a curious pair to produce a cookbook in tandem, since we still disagree about most cooking methods, and I often find her approach as infuriating as I guess she finds mine.

WHEN I was staying with her on Martha's Vineyard some fifteen years ago, we tried declaring a truce one afternoon by splitting a dinner into two parts. I was to go into the kitchen and cook the first part, with no comment from Lillian of any kind, and then I was to keep my mouth shut while she cooked the second part. When I went in, Lillian was sitting at the kitchen table smoking a cigarette. She smiled at me and said nothing. I went to work making some stuffed eggplants, New Orleans style, aware of the ominous silence behind me. I did not turn around.

"Forgive me," Lillian said, "but do you mean to be doing that?"

I said that I wouldn't be doing whatever I was doing if I didn't mean to be doing it.

"Do you realize how angry you sound?" Lillian said.

I gritted my teeth.

"You take criticism about writing very well," she said. "But not about cooking. Something seems to come over you when you cook. Something very childish."

She sat down and lit another cigarette.

I mixed the parboiled meat of the eggplant into the chopped vegetables and ham, peeled the shrimp, put the shells on the boil, and picked up the breadcrumbs, in silence.

"All I was going to say," Lillian said, "is that you always use too much olive oil."

I kept quiet and mixed in the breadcrumbs.

"I've long since believed that people who don't know their own angers are dangerous," Lillian said.

I put the spoon down and turned to face her. "Think of it this way," I said, "you don't know the difference between gumbo and stewed chicken."

"Are you saying I don't know how to cook New Orelans food?" Lillian asked in a dark voice.

I added that she didn't know Creole from Cajun.

"I'm not going to sit here and be insulted in my own kitchen," she said.

I pointed out that nobody had tied her to the chair.

Lillian rose with great dignity and stalked out. "Please knock on my door when you're finished," she said as she went, "I'll come down and cook the lamb."

There was the sound of a door slamming upstairs, then nothing.

I looked down, saw that there was too much olive oil in the pan, and added half a cup more.

Food to Fight Over

FIGHTING SOUP

Serves 6 to 8

2 small roasting chickens
1 veal knuckle
1 rutabaga
1 white turnip
2 parsnips
1 bunch parsley
2 cloves garlic
1 onion
1 clove
2 bay leaves

4 carrots
1 cup celery tops
1½ gallon water, cold

Cook all ingredients in water over low heat for 3 hours. Remove chicken and refrigerate for later use.

Strain soup, discarding vegetables, chill soup and skim off fat. Before serving, cube an additional ½ cup of each raw vegetable, add to soup, and simmer until vegetables are tender. Serve hot.

Food to Make Up a Fight

SORREL SOUP

Serves 6

1 onion, chopped
3 tablespoons butter
1 pound sorrel, cleaned and stemmed
4 tablespoons cream
2 cups chicken stock
1 egg yolk
2 tablespoons fresh lemon juice
1 teaspoon salt
¼ teaspoon pepepr
¼ teaspoon nutmeg

Cook onion in butter until soft. Add sorrel, cream and chicken stock and boil for 6 minutes. Puree mixture in food processor or blender until smooth. Return soup to pan. Combine egg yolk with lemon juice and whisk into soup. Return soup to very low heat (don't let it boil or egg will curdle) and season with salt, pepper and nutmeg. Serve hot or cold with a dollop of sour cream on top.

STUFFED EGGPLANT

Serves 6

3 medium-size eggplants
¼ cup olive oil

1 cup butter
¼ cup onions, minced
¼ cup scallions, minced
2 cloves garlic, minced
1 cup chopped tomatoes
½ teaspoon salt
½ teaspoon pepper
½ teaspoon cayenne pepper
½ teaspoon thyme
1 pound ham, ground
2 cups breadcrumbs
2 tablespoons parsley
½ pound shrimp, cleaned, chopped and lightly cooked

Preheat oven to 400 degrees. Slice eggplants in half lengthwise and hollow out. Save the pulp and chop. In a large skillet, heat olive oil and brown eggplant shells. Cover and cook for 5 minutes until shells begin to soften. Remove eggplant shells and drain olive oil. Melt butter in skillet. Add onion, scallions and garlic. Cook over low heat for 5 minutes. Add chopped eggplant pulp, tomatoes, salt, pepper, cayenne pepper and thyme and cook slowly until mixture thickens like a paste. Remove from heat. Add ground ham, breadcrumbs, parsley, and shrimp, if desired. Combine well. Put mixture into eggplant boats. Sprinkle lightly with additional breadcrumbs. Place an additional pat of butter on each boat. Place stuffed eggplants in a shallow baking dish and bake in 400-degree oven for 10 minutes until breadcrumbs toast and butter melts.

BROILED LEG OF LAMB

Serves 6

1 leg of lamb, butterflied
⅔ cup olive oil
2 tablespoons lemon juice
1 teaspoon salt
½ teaspoon pepper
½ cup parsley, minced
3 bay leaves

4 cloves garlic
¼ cup fresh rosemary or 2 tablespoons dried rosemary
1 tablespoon Worcestershire sauce
1 teaspoon cayenne pepper
1 cup chicken stock

Combine olive oil, lemon juice, salt, pepper, parsley, bay leaves, garlic, rosemary, Worcestershire sauce and cayenne to make marinade. Marinate lamb overnight, turning several times. Remove lamb from marinade one hour prior to cooking. Reserve marinade. Preheat broiler. Broil leg (shin side down) for 30 minutes. Turn. Broil for 15 additional minutes. Remove lamb from roasting pan. Add chicken stock to pan and scrape well to deglaze. Add ½ cup reserved marinade. Remove from heat. Taste and add additional salt and pepper, if needed. Slice the lamb, and serve the sauce separately.

SUGAR COOKIES

Yields 40 cookies

1 cup sugar
½ cup butter, softened
1 egg
1 teaspoon vanilla
1 teaspoon lemon extract or almond extract
⅓ cup sour cream
2 cups flour
⅓ teaspoon baking soda
¼ teaspoon salt

Beat together sugar and butter. Add egg, vanilla, lemon extract and sour cream. In a separate bowl, sift together flour, baking soda and salt. Combine butter mixture and flour mixture. Chill dough overnight. Preheat oven to 375 degrees. Roll dough very thin and cut with cookie cutter. Bake at 375 degrees for 8 minutes. Remove from tray immediately and serve with a bowl of fresh berries.

In those days I visited Lillian for all or part of every summer on the Vineyard. I was usually at work on a novel, and when I came down in the morning, no matter how early, fresh coffee was hot in a Silex on the stove and she was at her typewriter finishing work for the day.

As a rule, she was in a high good mood when she first woke up and her sense of well-being continued steadily until noon, at which time she began to think about subjects ranging from death to Hitler. I am the opposite. As soon as it begins to get sunless and dark out, I cheer up. Thinking about food in the morning, let alone planning menus, was as impossible for me as it was necessary for her, so mornings were tricky for both of us.

As a way of coping on especially bright and clear days, one of us would make a hot New Orleans breakfast of grillades and grits, and we would eat it without talking, while Lillian basked in the sun that poured through the windows and I got my mind unstuck. Grillades and grits are a fine way of waking up on any special day.

Food to Wake Up

GRILLADES AND GRITS

Serves 6

4 6-ounce veal steaks
1 cup flour
4 tablespoons butter
1 clove garlic, minced
1 green pepper, minced
2 onions, minced
2 stalks celery, minced
2 cups chicken stock
1 bay leaf
1½ cups canned tomatoes, chopped

1 tablespoon water
1 tablespoon cornstarch
1 cup hominy grits (Quaker brand)
additional water
salt and pepper

Season veal steaks with salt and pepper, dust in flour, and brown in butter in skillet. Remove veal to a warm platter and allow to rest at room temperature. Add garlic, green pepper, onion and celery to pan and cook briefly. Stir in chicken stock, bay leaf, tomatoes and simmer for one hour. Combine water (1 tablespoon) and cornstarch and whisk into mixture and simmer for 3 minutes. Add 5 cups water and 1 cup hominy grits. Simmer for 30 minutes. Add reserved veal and cook until warm. Serve grits with veal on top.

FOOD in America is often dismissed as the least important part of what Americans call "entertaining," a term that seems to mean feeding people. "Do you entertain a lot?" is genteel jargon for "Do you ask people to eat with you?," but too much attention is paid to who's asked and not enough to what's eaten. Perhaps in response to this mistake, Lilly tends to the opposite extreme.

One Monday morning on the Vineyard I came down to find her making a guest list for a dinner she was planning the following Saturday. This did not bode well. It left six days during which she was apt to change the menu maybe fifty times, settling on it only at the very last minute, so that around five P.M. on the Saturday in question she could begin to resent the people she had invited, because they had accepted her invitation and had to be fed.

Martha's Vineyard was a curious place for a dinner party: a guest list sounded like an exercise in name-dropping. As a general rule, nobody is as impressed by celebrities as other celebrities, and the covey of famous people on the island drifted from house to house, week to week, depending largely on who had the best weekend guest to be honored. Lillian was expecting Mike and Annabel Nichols, which was considered top of the line even in that rarified atmosphere. She was an expert at seating people, but most of her friends had heard each other's stories years before. By the end of July, Vineyard gossip was hard to come by, and by mid August a certain frantic quality began to set in.

"I think," Lillian said as I reached for the coffee, "I'll ask the Herseys, Anne and Art Buchwald, Kay Graham, Bob Brustein, Jules Feiffer, Bill and Rose Styron, Tony Lewis, Walter Cronkite, Lally Weymouth, Norman Mailer — he's staying with somebody for the weekend — and Teddy Kennedy, if he's with the Styrons. What do you think?"

I said I thought that would be fine.

"Okay," she said, "about the menu. Maybe I'll cook a simple pasta dish, and just have some salad and lemon sherbet. How does that sound?"

A few seconds went by.

"Please don't stare at me that way, Peter," she said. "There's lots of fresh basil in the garden. We could begin with spaghetti and diced tomatoes and basil. Okay?"

I said okay.

Lillian wrote it down, and then lifted the pencil and looked at it. "The trouble," she said thoughtfully, "is that I ordered fresh mussels last week from a fisherman I met. He said he'd deliver them Saturday morning, he's charging me almost nothing. We *can't* have mussels *and* spaghetti with basil. That's two first courses."

"So have the mussels," I said.

"Don't answer before you think," Lillian said. "If we have mussels, what am I going to do with all the basil in the garden? — What about *that?*"

I swallowed another half cup of coffee and said she could have them both if she put them together.

"You see?" Lilly said, brightening, "if you'd just try thinking once in a while your whole life would be different. Basil and mussel sauce." She wrote it down. "Do you think we should have it as a first course . . . or as a main course?" she added, setting herself up for an impossible choice.

"A main course," I said.

"That means we don't have any first course," Lillian said.

"Skip the first course," I said.

"What's the matter with you?" Lillian said, "you're too young to cave in like that. Why am I having such a problem with it?"

"You want the problem," I said, "you don't want the solution."

"Let's not have any Woolworth Freud," Lillian said, "let's stick to the menu."

I said nothing.

"So what's the first course?" Lillian said.

An hour and three menus later, she was struggling over a choice between mussels and bluefish.

When Saturday came she sat down in the same chair at five o'clock, dressed for the party, and said: "I don't see why all those people are coming to my house expecting me to feed them. It's your fault," she said to Mike, who was coming downstairs with Annabel. "I'm only doing this for you."

"I didn't want a party," Mike said gently; "I came to rest."

"That's no excuse and you know it," Lillian said, "getting this meal ready in time has taken ten years off my life. Nobody else on the island cares about food — they'll probably hate it."

I made some inane remark about nobody hating a good meal, and Mike said he was sure Lillian's guests would like whatever she served them.

"They should all be honored you invited them," Annabel said loyally.

"Fuck all of them," Lillian said, "except the Herseys. Let's have a drink."

The social mores of the artist-intellectual set on the Vineyard are the flip side of Easthampton, which is to say that a man who wears a tie is gauche, elegance is outré, discomfort a virtue, modesty a must, casual living reigns and nobody who has air-conditioning in a bedroom admits to it. Wealth is seldom displayed except in real estate, and frayed cuffs are chic. In all countries the rules of rebellion are more strict than what is being rebelled against (nobody is as judgmental as a bohemian) and the casual life on this part of the Vineyard is more rigidly mannered than its black-tie opposite. A hostess giving a formal Easthampton buffet might go the whole hog and have an ice-sculpture swan; but Lillian had to keep things looking like just folks. In an effort to keep it plain, she had stayed in the kitchen all day and I had made an ordinary chopped vegetable salad with one lone leftover radish stuck on top.

Just as the doorbell rang, Lillian took the radish off and buried it in the salad.

"You don't want people to think you're decorating food around here," she said. "Some of them would never speak to you again."

Food for a Modest, Unmoveable Feast

CHOPPED VEGETABLE SALAD

Serves 6

1 zucchini, cut into bite-size pieces
2 carrots, cut into bite-size pieces and lightly blanched
2 cups green beans, cleaned, cut into bite-size pieces and blanched
1 red pepper, chopped
1 green pepper, chopped
2 stalks celery, chopped
1 bunch scallions, chopped
1 bunch radishes, sliced thin
2 packages frozen mixed vegetables
2 cups Romescu sauce (recipe follows)

Combine all vegetables in a large bowl. Toss with 2 cups Romescu sauce. Refrigerate and serve well chilled.

ROMESCU SAUCE

1½ cups

¼ cup almonds, toasted
1 clove garlic
½ teaspoon cayenne pepper
1 teaspoon salt
1 tomato, peeled, seeded and chopped
¼ cup red wine vinegar
1 cup olive oil

Pulverize almonds, garlic, cayenne pepper, salt, tomato and vinegar in blender. Slowly drizzle in oil, making sure that each addition is completely absorbed. Adjust seasoning to taste with additional salt and pepper.

PASTA WITH BASIL AND TOMATOES

Serves 6

1 cup olive oil
2 cloves garlic, minced
12 tomatoes, peeled, seeded and chopped
1 bunch fresh basil leaves, minced
salt and pepper
2 pounds pasta (angel hair or vermicelli)
grated Parmesan cheese

Heat olive oil in a large skillet. Add garlic and cook until it begins to turn golden. Add tomatoes and basil and continue cooking over medium heat until warmed. Season with salt and pepper to taste. Cook 2 pounds thin pasta. Drain, toss with sauce, adding up to 1 additional cup of olive oil to coat. Sprinkle with grated Parmesan cheese and serve.

LILLIAN is good at leaving food outside the door of any writer who is working, and over a period spanning a decade and a half of Vineyard summers, she never once said to me the thing all people (even other writers) say to writers: "You have to stop for lunch." There is, of course, no such thing as lunch, unless you want there to be; and I mostly didn't. If I kept my door closed, which was sometimes the case, she left a tray outside, knocked once and went away.

Food to Leave Outside a Door

CHICKEN-STUFFED BAKED TOMATOES

Serves 6

2 pounds chicken meat, cooked and cut coarsely
¼ pound smoked ham
6 tomatoes, hollowed out, with pulp reserved
3 tablespoons butter
1 cup chopped onions
½ cup chopped parsley
1 bay leaf
¼ teaspoon thyme
¼ teaspoon pepper
½ teaspoon salt
½ cup breadcrumbs

Preheat oven 350 degrees. Grind cooked chicken meat with smoked ham. Place hollowed tomatoes in lightly oiled baking dish. Melt butter in skillet and cook onions until soft. Add tomato pulp, parsley, bay leaf, thyme, pepper and salt and cook over low heat until thick. Add chicken, ham and breadcrumbs. Mix well and season to taste with additional salt and pepper. Stuff tomatoes and sprinkle with additional breadcrumbs and top each with a pat of butter. Bake for 45 minutes in 350-degree oven.

LOBSTER AND SHRIMP SALAD

Serves 4

2 quarts water
1 tablespoon salt
1 bay leaf
¼ cup wine vinegar
1 onion, quartered
1 teaspoon olive oil
2 2-pound lobsters
2 pounds shrimp
1½ cups chopped lettuce
1 tomato, peeled, seeded and chopped
½ cup onions, minced
2 hard-cooked eggs, chopped
½ cup homemade mayonnaise (recipe page 27)

Combine 2 quarts water, quartered onion, olive oil, salt, bay leaf and vinegar and bring to a boil. Add lobster and steam for 10 minutes. Add shrimp and steam for another 5 minutes. Drain and cool shellfish under cold water. Clean and chop the lobster and shrimp into bite-size pieces. Toss well-cooled lobster, shrimp, chopped lettuce, chopped tomato, minced onion and chopped hard-cooked eggs with mayonnaise and serve.

ONCE in a while we would drive up-island from Lillian's house in Vineyard Haven to a tiny dilapidated one-room shack on a small piece of mosquito-ridden marsh which she referred to as "the Gay Head Property." The beach at Gay Head was wide and very long, the largest nude beach on the island, and Lillian's gray wooden shack abutted a sand dune facing it. She kept the shack carefully padlocked, and every year some couple broke in and used it as a place to have sex, usually without stealing anything because there was nothing to steal save a rusty beach chair and a beach umbrella that had never worked.

A rocky dirt road lead to the Gay Head Property and there was a large metal gate with another padlock, the gate partially covered by signs reading "PRIVATE," "PLEASE STAY OUT," "THIS MEANS YOU" and "PROPERTY OWNERS ONLY," this last referring to two shacks much like Lillian's, one deserted and the other with laundry hanging out to dry. When we reached the Gay Head Property, I would get out of the car, unlock the gate, drive in, park, get out, and lock the gate again. There were always four or five cars already there, since anybody who wanted a key seemed to have one, and Lillian would make some remark about people having no respect for privacy while we walked a thin sand path through the marsh to her shack, took out the second key, and found that it wasn't necessary because the door was already open. We left our picnic lunch on the porch and went down to the water where she covered herself from head to toe with a beach towel and took off her bathing suit under it.

Modesty has its own rules, I guess, and I tried explaining to Lillian many times that it is not in the nature of people who wish to become naked to cover themselves up in order to do so: for the same price, she could have stood up and stripped. "You don't understand," was all she ever said, squirming under the towel for several minutes until she emerged, nude, and walked into the ocean. All around her, naked people who were sitting or lying down, watched this process with a certain curiosity.

There is a special sort of tilt to a naked beach picnic, and not everybody is equipped to handle it. You have to pack things well, you have to unpack them better, you have to watch where you sit. Above all you have to know which are the tastes that improve in sunlight, in a salt breeze, with the great tainted iodine smell of the ocean, and which aren't. Beef stew, for instance, is not a good idea — I don't know why, it just isn't. Last night's leftovers can be fine, depending on what you do to fix them up, but all food is not suited to all weathers and not everything tastes good under the sun.

Food for a Beach Picnic

GUACAMOLE

Serves 6

3 ripe avocados
2 cloves garlic, minced
¼ cup fresh minced coriander
2 tablespoons fresh lime juice
dash of Louisiana hot sauce
salt and pepper to taste

Peel and pit the avocado and mash the pulp. Add garlic, coriander and lime juice. Add hot sauce, salt and pepper to taste. Mix well and serve with taco chips.

HUMMUS

Serves 6

3 cups chick-peas, drained
3 cloves garlic
1 cup tahini
1½ teaspoons salt
2 teaspoons lemon juice
raw vegetable crudités

Combine first five ingredients in a blender and puree until smooth. Adjust seasoning with additional salt and lemon juice to taste and serve with raw vegetable crudités.

People who want to make a special occasion of beach-eating can't do a lot better than a formal New England clambake, served up in layers. Unfortunately a clambake is one of the things you have to do right or not do at all, and doing it right takes all day. We sometimes debated having a clambake instead of a sit-down dinner, for this person or that person, until Lillian declared over her second martini one afternoon that she didn't like anybody that much and we might as well have it ourselves.

The next day we gave it a go, cutting down on some of the more complicated procedures until we arrived at a kind of ersatz small clambake that pleased us enough to repeat it about once a year from then on.

CLAMBAKE FOR TWO

4 links Linguica sausage
2 small white onions, peeled
4 small white potatoes
4 ears sweet corn
12 littleneck clams, well scrubbed
3 cups white wine
2 1-pound lobsters

In a large pot, layer the sausage, onions, potatoes, corn and clams. Add the white wine. Cover the pot and bring it to a boil. Add the lobster and cook for 15 minutes. Check potatoes and clams, lower flame, and continue cooking until potatoes are tender and clams are open. Spread the table with newspaper and lay out a supply of paper towels. Serve the clambake right from the pot with plenty of drawn butter and some cold beer.

FOOD that is good on sand is not necessarily the same as food that is good on water. Every couple of weeks on the Vineyard, John and Barbara Hersey would take us out on John's boat. John is a great sailor, Barbara Hersey a beautiful woman who cooks a good steak sandwich. Once in a while you meet somebody who knows how to cook something you can't learn; it took me five summers to get Barbara's steak sandwich right and

I still can't make it taste the way she can. I like to think that the sea helps it a little. Something does exist in New England waters, something hard to define. I remember our last boat trip very well. While John and Lillian stood up and fished, back to back on opposite sides of the boat, now and then tangling their lines deep in the water and yanking at each other like two affectionate members of a faintly demented comedy team, Barbara broke open the sandwiches and the world seemed a much better and safer place than it is.

Food for a Boat

BARBARA HERSEY'S SLICED STEAK SANDWICH

In order to make Hersey's sliced steak sandwiches, cover the bottom of an iron skillet with ⅛ inch of oil, heat it till it's smoking, and cook the steak about 3 minutes on each side. Take it out and slice it thin. Use thin rye bread for the sandwich.

That's all Barbara does.

There are two tricks: (1) Leap back when you put the steak in the skillet or you will burn any exposed part of your body, as I did, and (2) open all windows and doors in the kitchen or you will die of smoke inhalation.

ONE of the tastes I like best is almost anything cooked outdoors in the back yard. Lillian's back yard is a garden that leads to a beach overlooking the boats on the Vineyard Haven Bay, but any space that will hold a grill will serve the same purpose.

Grilled food is a specialty act for most cooks. A pungent marinade or a good barbecue sauce makes a lot of difference, as does some knowledge of fire itself. Frenchmen in South America invented the term barbecue, which meant spitting a whole animal, beard to tail *(de barbe à cue)* over open flames. Most North American cooks use only a small part of any land animal, and the spit has gone out of fashion for home use. Charcoal is the order of the day, but nobody bothers with kindling since the advent of starter-fluid, which seems to me a shame, in that people douse the coals with so much fluid the food often tastes like kerosene. With the manufacture of self-starting coals the whole business of outdoor cooking is a fast-food process that loses, I think, its main virtue. Good food should take time, either in the preparation or in the cooking. When I first took to using an outdoor grill, I was in too much of a hurry: the fire was always too high when I put the food on, and the coals weren't ready until about twenty minutes after everybody had eaten.

As a rule, whatever kind of coal you use, you want to make sure there is no visible fire when you start to cook, and you want to keep some water nearby, preferably in a spray can, in case the dripping fat rekindles the flame. If you happen to have a large pot or a patch of earth you can grow herbs in, a couple of fresh rosemary branches thrown over the coals can be wonderful, especially in the grilling of lamb.

If the weather suits, my idea of a good birthday dinner is plain grill food, and every August on the Vineyard when my birthday came around I would marinate some kind of meat, light the coals, sit outside with Lillian, and uncork a bottle of wine. I happen to hate champagne, but a good red Bordeaux is my idea of a celebration.

There is a jetty in the water off Lillian's beach, a protected area where small boats are anchored. In the evening you can hear the tinkling of the bells on top of the masts as if the fireflies had voices, and across the water the lights from Oak Bluffs look like dingy unwashed stars. The Vineyard ferry comes and goes past the house, all lit up, and the iron odor of seaweed mingles with the sizzling smells from the grill. If you like to swim at night, a turn on the beach just before the food is ready is a good thing.

Food for an Outdoor Grill

MARINATED LAMB CHOPS

Serves 6

½ cup olive oil
1 cup white wine
4 bay leaves, crumbled
4 cloves garlic, minced
2 onions, sliced thin
1 tablespoon mustard
12 lamb chops, cut about 1½ inches thick
salt and pepper

Combine olive oil, white wine, bay leaves, garlic, onion and mustard to make marinade. Marinate lamb for 2 hours, turning frequently. Remove lamb from marinade. Season with kosher salt and black pepper. Grill over charcoal for 5 minutes on one side, basting several times with marinade. Turn lamb chops, baste, and broil on second side for 4–7 minutes depending on how you like your lamb cooked.

GRILLED VEGETABLE KABOBS

Serves 6

1 large head of broccoli, cleaned and cut into six sections
½ cup lemon juice
1 clove garlic, minced
¼ cup olive oil
1 teaspoon salt
½ teaspoon black pepper
2 eggplants, cut into 1½-inch cubes

Steam broccoli for 3 minutes. Drain and cool completely under cold water. Combine lemon juice, garlic, olive oil, salt and pepper.

Toss broccoli and raw, cubed eggplant in lemon mixture and marinate for one hour. Arrange six skewers with broccoli stalk sandwiched between eggplant cubes and grill over charcoal until tender.

GRILLED PINEAPPLE

Serves 6

2 ripe pineapples, peeled and cut into ¾-inch slices
1 cup brown sugar

Sprinkle pineapple with brown sugar one hour before cooking. When coals are dying down, brush excess sugar from pineapple slices and brown the slices on each side. Serve with vanilla ice cream.

ONE evening the summer before last, I noticed Lillian staring off into space with a look I didn't recognize. She had by then developed glaucoma — her eyesight was badly impaired — and she couldn't see at all after sunset; but on this night she seemed to be watching an object a great distance away, as if it were coming closer in the darkness. I asked her what the matter was.

"I'm not sure," Lillian said in a flat way. Since her first stroke she had had trouble standing up. "I wonder if I'll make it like this till September."

"By 'make it' you mean stay vertical?"

"I mean stay alive," Lillian said.

It was late August and she was in a strange mood. I put it down to the fact of the summer ending and went on with my work on the grill.

After a very long time, Lillian said:

"What kind of food did you eat growing up?"

"Where?" I said. "New Orleans or Spain?"

"Anywhere," she said. Then after a moment: "Let's talk about food. . . ."

2

New Orleans

I GREW up in New Orleans when people who lived there referred to the place by one of its four main sections: uptown, downtown, back-of-town and out of town. First we had a house downtown in the French Quarter, till I was five, then we lived in my grandparents' house, uptown, while my parents got an architect to build us a house in a suburb called Metairie, out of town. I would lie in bed at night in the new house and listen to the freight trains chug off and fade with a wheeze that was quick and soft and violent. The sound is still hard for me to describe because I used to think it was the sound of goodbye.

New Orleans food requires some explaining. The city resembles a Mediterranean port town, and Creole and Cajun food together form a complex cuisine that doesn't exist anyplace else.

In other parts of America, New Orleans terminology is often misinterpreted. The word *Creole* is a good example — it does not mean mulatto. Creole simply refers to a group of colonists and their descendants who maintain some of the customs and language of the mother country. Creoles can be any nationality, but in New Orleans they were mostly French and Spanish.

After the Creoles, another invasion hit South Louisiana: the Cajuns, a large colony of French Huguenots who had been expelled from Nova Scotia and had wandered the coastline of the

American colonies for a decade, rejected everywhere till they found a place nobody else wanted — the marshes and swamps of South Louisiana.

While Creole cooking aspires to an aristocratic *grande cuisine,* the Cajuns tend to serve strong country food, pungent and peppery, often cooked together in the same pot, tamed by a bed of white rice.

Where Creole and Cajun cuisines blend, you find the best of Louisiana cooking, and you can trace the history of New Orleans in the evolution of any one of its most famous dishes. There is, for instance, gumbo. The first French Creole settlers in Louisiana brought with them a taste for bouillabaisse, but there was no *rascasse* (a Mediterranean fish) in local waters — no lobster or eels. So the early Creoles substituted blue crabs from Lake Pontchartrain along with shrimp, oysters, red snapper and pompano from the Gulf of Mexico. After that, the Cajuns showed the Creoles how to do it with shellfish alone, using only crab and shrimp. Spanish settlers contributed red peppers, grown on Avery Island west of New Orleans. Black Africans came in with okra, while the local American Indians showed everybody the use of filé powder — ground sassafras leaves. The result, New Orleans gumbo, is at least as good as the original bouillabaisse.

If you ask a South Louisiana cook for a single rule to use as a guide in both Creole and Cajun cooking, you will be told to "start with a roux." After that you're on your own. A roux is made of fat — oil or lard or butter — mixed with flour in a pot over a flame. It's tricky to make because it can burn and turn black in a second, and once it does you have to throw it out and start over. A good roux should be brown, about the color of ordinary dark commercial maple syrup. The instant you get the right color you throw in the next ingredients to stop the burning, and the cooking begins.

The most recent French public relations hard-sell, *nouvelle cuisine,* hit New Orleans with a wet thud and was rejected accordingly. After a while, one or two of the *nouvelle cuisine* rules snuck into town more quietly and one day Commander's Palace, my favorite of the city's elegant restaurants, stopped using a roux in its gumbo. This did not go unnoticed. Commander's *nouvelle* gumbo was mumbled about, discussed, shunned — and then accepted.

Nothing that can be eaten or drunk in New Orleans is ever taken lightly. The last time I went back for a visit, an old friend warned me, in somber tones, of two "new dangers" in the city.

"The unlit section of St. Ann Street has muggers at night," he said gloomily, "and the wine they serve in that new Metairie steak house is suicide."

New Orleans cooks tend to have personal kitchen quirks that don't always go into recipes. I, for instance, don't like to use plain water if I can avoid it. Water seems to me to leach out flavor and add nothing, so I'll use stock, wine, beer or even fruit juice if I can. I seldom add salt to food if I can find salt pork or something else containing a salty tang. For that purpose, I buy prosciutto bones, saw them into 3-inch pieces, and keep them in the freezer. I use the bone segments instead of salt for all soups, stews, casseroles and some vegetable dishes. As an additional quirk, in certain recipes for soup or stew where garlic is called for, I usually throw the whole head in, without peeling it, removing only the dry outer skin with my hands. When the dish is almost done, I press the cooked head of garlic against the inside of the pot with the back of a wooden spoon and then discard the empty remains. Curiously, this does not increase the taste of garlic by much, but it does enrich the overall flavor. The above eccentricities should be kept in mind as optional substitutions in all the following recipes, whether they're from New Orleans, Spain or elsewhere.

If you're having a pompous gourmet to dinner, gumbo, I think, is a good main dish. Almost nobody who isn't from New Orleans serves it decently, and Northern cooks tend to fiddle with it for some reason. Gumbo should be served either in soup bowls or in individual casserole dishes with lids; and it ought to be put on the table before people sit down. White rice can be passed separately or served on the side so that each person can add the amount he wants. Filé powder can be added (optionally) just before serving, and you want to be careful not to overdo filé — too much of it gives gumbo a ropy texture. I like okra gumbo better myself, but here are both recipes:

Food for a Gourmet

SHRIMP, HAM AND OKRA GUMBO

Serves 6

2 pounds shrimp
2 tablespoons bacon fat
1 pound okra, cut into ¼-inch slices
2 cloves garlic, minced
1 onion, chopped
1 teaspoon thyme
2 bay leaves
1 fresh chili pepper, minced
1 teaspoon black pepper
2 tablespoons brown roux (see below)
1 cup tomatoes, peeled and chopped
¼ pound smoked ham, cut into bit-size cubes
salt to taste

Peel shrimp and boil shells in 12 cups of water for 30 minutes. Strain, discard shells, and reserve stock. In a large casserole, melt bacon fat, add okra and cook for 5 minutes. Add garlic, onion, thyme, bay leaves, chili pepper and black pepper and cook for 5 more minutes. Add brown roux and stir. Add 8 cups reserved shrimp stock and tomatoes. Bring mixture to a boil. Reduce heat. Add ham and simmer for 45 minutes, adding additional stock or water if necessary. Add shrimp and cook for 15 additional minutes. Adjust seasoning with salt and pepper. Serve with cooked rice.

Brown Roux

Yields 1½ cups

1 cup all-purpose flour
1 cup vegetable oil

Combine flour and oil in a heavy skillet over the lowest heat possible. Stir the ingredients with a metal spatula to make a smooth paste. Continue cooking over very low heat, stirring frequently to avoid burning. The roux will darken to a rich, dark brown in 30 to 45 minutes. As it begins to darken, watch the mixture carefully because this is the time it may burn. When dark brown, remove roux from heat and scrape into a small bowl. Allow to cool. Cover and store in refrigerator for later use.

SHRIMP, SAUSAGE AND CHICKEN GUMBO FILÉ

Serves 6

1½ pounds shrimp
1 2- to 3-pound chicken, cut up
3 tablespoons brown roux (see above)
1 onion, chopped
1 red pepper, chopped
1 green pepper, chopped
1 chili pepper, minced
2 bay leaves
1 teaspoon thyme
1 pound Andouille (or other smoked, spicy sausage), minced
3 teaspoons filé powder

Shell shrimp and boil shells in 12 cups of water for 30 minutes. Strain, discard shells, and reserve stock. In a separate pot, cover chicken with water and simmer for 45 minutes. Remove chicken. Combine shrimp broth and chicken broth and boil to reduce to about ½ gallon. Set aside. Melt roux in a large, heavy-bottom casserole.

Add onion, peppers, bay leaves and thyme. Cook slowly until vegetables are soft. Then add 4 cups reserved stock and minced sausage. Simmer for one hour, adding more stock as necessary. Add cleaned shrimp and reserved chicken. Simmer for 15 additional minutes. Adjust seasoning with salt and pepper. Add filé powder. Stir well and serve immediately.

THERE are about thirty-six food festivals a year in South Louisiana, and special occasions in New Orleans, when they have to do with food, happen at least once a week. Sunday is traditionally a day for serving ham, which makes Monday the day for red beans and rice all over town, because the leftover ham bone can be cracked and put in the beans while they're cooking. The marrow inside the ham bone gives the beans a silky texture that's hard to come by any other way.

I've never liked *haute cuisine* as much as peasant food in any country. Red beans and rice is strictly peasant food, and I happen to prefer it to almost any other New Orleans dish. It's rich and pungent in taste, inexpensive to make and nourishing: red beans eaten with rice form a whole protein. It should be served New Orleans style, with some white vinegar on the side, allowing each person to add a splash to taste.

Food for a Monday Special

RED BEANS AND RICE

Serves 6

1 pound dried red beans
6 cups water
4 tablespoons bacon fat or lard
1 cup scallions, minced
1 cup onions, minced
½ cup celery, minced

3 cloves garlic, minced
½ cup green pepper, minced
2 pounds smoked ham hock
½ teaspoon black pepper
3 cups cooked white rice

Add beans to water and boil for 5 minutes. Remove from heat and allow to soak for one hour. Melt bacon fat in a casserole, add ham hock, scallions, onions, celery, garlic and green pepper and cook until vegetables are soft. Add beans and liquid and cook, partially covered, for 3 hours. Add more water as necessary and stir frequently. Serve on white rice along with a cruet of white vinegar.

MEMORIES of childhood are often filtered through a different perception, a distorting lens, like something seen under water. Now and then I can connect events to tastes, sometimes to food itself — like being in the kitchen one hot sticky afternoon when the cook made her version of Daube Glacé and set it in the icebox to chill. (For "icebox" please read "refrigerator" from here on. New Orleans people didn't use the latter word when I grew up, and I never got used to it.) We often left town in the summer to get out of the heat, but this summer, I think, must have been an exception, because I remember kitchen talk about the Fourth of July and what it meant. What it meant was cold food.

There is a theory creeping around the North which would lead you to believe that cold food all tastes more or less the same. It doesn't. Daube Glacé is a flamboyant main dish of sliced jellied beef and vegetables, with enough hot spices in the cooking to give it anything from a tingle to a whiplash. The contrast of spice-hot and ice-cold does something to counteract the heat of July and August better than almost any dish I know.

For a good summer dessert, I remember best our cook's version of Ambrosia. She started with half a watermelon sliced lengthwise and hollowed out. Into the empty shell she put layers of as many different fruits as she could get her hands on: three kinds of melon balls, grapes, slices of orange and tangerine, mango, papaya, berries of all sorts, sliced bananas and peaches and apples and pears and plums, an occasional layer of fresh grated coconut and then more fresh fruit, till the melon shell was heaped high. Sometimes she added a few finely chopped mint leaves, sometimes not. She chilled the Ambrosia in the icebox till time to serve, then she broke open a bottle of champagne and poured it over the whole thing. There was something festive about it and fun, not unlike the fireworks that glittered overhead on the Fourth, sparkle to match sparkle.

Food for the Fourth of July

DAUBE GLACÉ

Yields 2 loaves

7 tablespoons vegetable oil
4 pounds beef shinbones, sawed into 1-inch lengths
4 pounds veal shinbones, sawed into 1-inch lengths
3 medium-size onions, chopped
2 stalks celery, chopped
3 carrots, chopped
2 pounds pigs' feet
4 sprigs parsley
5 quarts water
5 pounds bottom round beef, 3 equal pieces
1 carrot, grated
3 cloves garlic
1 red pepper, minced
1 lemon rind, minced
2 teaspoons salt
1 teaspoon cayenne pepper
1 onion, sliced

Prepare 24 hours in advance. In a skillet heat 4 tablespoons of oil and brown the beef and veal bones. Pour off all but 2 tablespoons of fat. Add chopped onions, celery and 3 chopped carrots. Cook 10 minutes. Put vegetables and bones in stock pot, add pigs' feet and parsley. Add 5 quarts of water and boil. Simmer for 4 hours. Discard bones and pigs' feet. Strain stock. Add 2 tablespoons of oil to the skillet and brown the beef. Transfer to 10-quart casserole. Pour stock over beef. Cover with liquid. Bring to a boil and simmer 3½ hours. Strain stock and cut beef into ½-inch chunks. Combine beef in bowl with grated carrots, garlic, red pepper, lemon, salt, cayenne pepper, and toss. Put in icebox. Skim fat off stock. Put in icebox for 2 hours. Warm stock and put ¼-inch layer of stock into the bottoms of two loaf pans (9x5x3). Put in icebox to form jelly. Dip sliced onion in remaining liquid stock and arrange 3 slices in bottom of each loaf pan. Chill. Pour all the remaining liquid stock over the beef and mix. Ladle into loaf pans. Put in icebox for 12 hours. Scrape off fat. Carefully unmold.

NEW ORLEANS has become one of the convention meccas of the world — yet even ten thousand members of the American Medical Association at one time have little effect on the availability of restaurants to locals. Many of the bigger restaurants have a private hotline for New Orleans residents and some have separate entrances. I had a great-uncle named Max who used to take me out to dinner once a month when I was ten as a kind of culinary indoctrination.

Uncle Max had his own table and his own waiter in each of the restaurants he frequented, a tradition still alive in New Orleans. "You can't let an unknown waiter serve you," Uncle Max said; "it would be like eating on the floor." Once when I met him for dinner at the Caribbean Room of the Hotel Pontchartrain, I got there a few minutes late to find him gently dozing on the floor under the table. "Your great-uncle is having himself a nap," the unruffled waiter said. "He had an extra martini while he was waiting for you . . . he won't sleep long, he never does . . . would you care for something to eat till he wakes up?"

In New Orleans restaurants, I still like to eat two or even three appetizers and skip the main course. Baked oysters of three kinds — Bienville, Rockefeller, and Roffignac — are good. So are shrimp remoulade, crawfish bisque and turtle soup, all specialties of the city. New Orleans turtle soup has nothing in common with the watery variety served elsewhere. It's thick as tropical mud and, if you're lucky, it has a couple of turtle eggs floating in it. If your dinner guests are foreigners, any New Orleans appetizer is good: Europeans tend to be snobbish about American cooking and they forget that much of it originated in Europe.

A warning: baked oysters are served on a bed of blistering rock salt to retain the heat and to keep the shells from tipping. It's best to explain this to people, so they won't try to eat it. If a foreigner gets a forkful of hot rock salt into his mouth before you can stop him, he's a goner. I almost lost an Englishman that way.

Food for Snobbish Foreigners

OYSTERS BIENVILLE

Serves 4

2 dozen oysters, shucked, with liquid reserved; save bottom shells
1 pound shrimp, cleaned
2 pounds mushrooms
6 slices bacon, chopped
1 bunch scallions, chopped
½ cup parsley, chopped
1 clove garlic
4 tablespoons butter
1 cup flour

2 cups milk
½ cup American sauterne
¼ cup lemon juice
1 teaspoon cayenne pepper
4 egg yolks
salt
rock salt

Preheat oven to 350 degrees. Spread rock salt, about ½ inch deep, in four 9-inch pie pans. Sauté shrimp, mushrooms, bacon, scallions, parsley and garlic in butter for 5 minutes. Add flour, reserved oyster liquid, milk and sauterne. Simmer for 5 minutes. Remove from heat. Add lemon juice, 1 teaspoon salt, and cayenne pepper. Run mixture through a blender to make a smooth puree. Beat in 4 egg yolks. Arrange oysters in their shells on top of rock salt. Spoon sauce over oyster and bake for 15 minutes.

OYSTERS ROCKEFELLER

Serves 6

3 dozen oysters, shucked, with liquid reserved; save bottom shells
3 cups scallions
3 cups parsley
2 pounds spinach, chopped into 1-inch pieces
½ pound butter
4 cloves garlic
3 tablespoons anchovy paste
¾ teaspoon cayenne papper
1½ teaspoon salt
¾ cup Pernod
rock salt

Preheat oven to 350 degrees. Spread rock salt, about ½ inch deep, in six 9-inch pie pans. Put scallions, parsley and spinach through a meat grinder. Melt butter in pan and add garlic and oyster liquid. Bring to a boil. Stir in anchovy paste, cayenne pepper and salt. Add vegetables. Simmer 10 minutes. Add Pernod. Remove from heat. Arrange oysters in their shells on top of rock salt in baking pans. Spoon sauce over each oyster and bake for 15 minutes.

OYSTERS ROFFIGNAC

Serves 4

2 dozen oysters, shucked, with liquid reserved; save bottom shells
1 pound raw shrimp
½ pound mushrooms
1 cup onions, chopped
1 cup scallions, chopped
5 teaspoons garlic
½ pound butter
¼ cup flour
½ cup red wine
¼ cup tomato puree
1½ teaspoons cayenne pepper
1 teaspoon salt
rock salt

Preheat oven to 400 degrees. Spread rock salt about ½-inch deep in four 9-inch pie pans. Put on baking sheets and heat in oven. Drain oysters. Save about ½ cup of the liquid. Scrub and dry shells. Clean and pat dry shrimp. Add them to mushrooms, onions, scallions and garlic. Melt butter in a skillet. Add shrimp mixture and cook for 5 minutes. Add flour. Pour in wine, tomato puree and ½ cup oyster liquid. Cook and simmer for 3 minutes. Stir in cayenne pepper and salt. Toss in blender and puree. Put oyster shells on top of rock salt, place an oyster in each, and spoon sauce over each oyster. Bake 15 minutes.

SHRIMP REMOULADE

Serves 6

¼ cup strong mustard
2 tablespoons paprika
1 teaspoon cayenne pepper
3 teaspoons salt
½ cup tarragon vinegar
1¼ cups olive oil

1½ cups scallions, chopped
½ cup parsley
½ cup celery, chopped
3 pounds shrimp, cleaned
lettuce

Combine the mustard, paprika, cayenne pepper and salt. Beat in the tarragon vinegar. Add the olive oil and beat until thick. Add the scallions, parsley and celery. Cover and let it rest for 4 hours. Boil the shrimp and cool. Serve the shrimp cold on lettuce with the sauce on top.

TURTLE SOUP

Serves 6

2 pounds fresh or frozen turtle meat
1 onion, quartered
1 bay leaf
½ teaspoon cayenne pepper
2 teaspoons salt
1 cup butter
1 onion, chopped
½ cup flour
½ cup canned tomato puree
1 teaspoon Worcestershire sauce
½ cup sherry
2 hard-cooked eggs, chopped
1 tablespoon parsley, minced
lemon slices

Simmer turtle meat in 2 quarts of water along with quartered onion, bay leaf, cayenne pepper and 2 teaspoons of salt for 2 hours. Strain, reserve 6 cups of the liquid, and chop the meat into bite-size cubes. Melt butter and add chopped onion and cook until soft. Whisk in flour and continue cooking over low heat until brown. Add 4 cups of the reserved stock and bring to a boil. Reduce heat. Add tomato puree and Worcestershire sauce, and simmer for 10 minutes. Add meat, eggs and parsley. Season to taste with salt and pepper. Serve garnished with lemon slices.

NEW ORLEANS cooking is useful in many situations, as are certain New Orleans manners and social mores, ranging from food to sex. If you have in mind seducing someone with a meal, I would offer the following for consideration:

Whether you're male or female, never make a pass at anybody. The best pass is no pass at all. Extreme attention along with a look of helplessness works wonders, especially when accompanied by good food. The idea that you're willing to cook your heart out in silence has a tendency to touch people, with the possible exception of Lillian, and cooking is a form of attention that is considered more delicate than groping. Two recipes have been in my family for as long as I can remember, thanks to my oldest friend, Louise Phillips. Choose either one of them for purposes of seduction. Presenting both at the same meal would be considered overshooting the field.

Food for Seduction

OYSTER PIE

Serves 2

pastry dough for one-crust 9-inch pie
4 slices bacon
¼ cup onion, chopped
½ cup scallions, chopped
¼ cup parsley, chopped
½ teaspoon cayenne pepper
1 quart oysters, shucked and drained
butter

Preheat oven to 375 degrees. In a skillet, fry the bacon until crisp. Drain the bacon and crumble it. Add the onion to the bacon fat and cook until soft. Remove from heat and scrape the onion into a bowl.

Add the crumbled bacon, scallions, parsley and cayenne and mix together. Add the oysters and mix gently. Brush a 9-inch pie plate with butter, then add the oyster filling. Top with the rolled-out pie crust dough and prick it with a fork. Bake for 30 to 40 minutes.

CRÈME BRÛLÉE

Serves 2

2 cups heavy cream, warmed
2 teaspoons vanilla
4 egg yolks
1 cup granulated sugar

Preheat oven to 300 degrees. Beat egg yolks in bowl. Add 3 tablespoons of sugar and continue beating until creamy and light. Mix in the cream slowly, and the vanilla. Pour into a shallow glass dish. Place in the pan of water and bake in a 300-degree oven. Test with a toothpick after 30 minutes. When the toothpick comes out clean, remove the custard and refrigerate. It will become firm in about an hour. Cook remaining sugar with 3 tablespoons of water until you have caramel syrup. Pour the hot syrup evenly and thinly over the surface of the custard (to form a hard crust). Put back in the icebox until ready to serve.

WHEN I was ten, I used to take the streetcar downtown in the morning and back in the afternoon, skirting around on my way home to visit an Italian family that lived uptown near the Garden District. I would go slow whenever I walked there, a little bit awed by the place. Built by the first Anglo-Americans who came to Louisiana after the Purchase of 1803, the houses in the Garden District are big and ornate, wrapped in acres of azalea bushes, waxy-leafed magnolia trees, crape myrtle, gardenias so white you can't look at them in the sun, camellias of all colors, oleanders, jasmine, huge shiny green leaves called elephant ears, twisting vines and other flowers. Most of the cast-iron fences there end in old brick walls, enclosing each house in a kind of perfumed privacy.

The Italian family I went to see lived several blocks past the uptown edge of the District, in a very small house with their own grocery store on the first floor, no yard, and no garden at all. I remember sitting in their kitchen one day next to a pair of blowsy camellias in a jelly jar, eating some spaghetti Mrs. Cannetti had dished out for me. Her son Joey was my age and he waited with his arms crossed till I got through eating and we could go play.

The pasta sauces Mrs. Cannetti served were both Cajun and Creole, and she was good at concocting her own version of any local dish. Like other Italians in the city, she made an elaborate altar on March 19, St. Joseph's Day, which she took off from Lent as a kind of special occasion. Her altar was built in tiers of food — everything she could prepare from stuffed crab to stuffed artichokes, stuffed peppers, baked fish, shrimp, nuts, crawfish, alligator pears, fruits of all varieties, vegetables from squash to beans, bowls of antipasto, bottles of wine, pastries and syrups — all set around a statue of St. Joseph, with candles and banks of real and artificial flowers, a glitter of Christmas tree ornaments and strings of electric lights. Visitors who came to pay homage to the Saint were given a chunk of bread and a lucky bean and they left a couple of coins. If you kept the chunk of St. Joseph's Day bread inside your house all year, Mrs. Cannetti said it was a guarantee that you wouldn't starve, and her lucky beans were prized by many people — among them two gamblers who helped pay for her altar. I never did understand how you could carry on like that with food in the middle of Lent, but Mrs. Cannetti said my not understanding was all right considering I was Jewish, and she usually gave me a stuffed artichoke.

(I once cooked a stuffed artichoke for Lillian on St. Joseph's Day, after I grew up, and she suggested I add a little pastrami to the stuffing just to make things kosher.)

On regular days when I went to visit, Joey and I would play on the levee and Mrs. Cannetti gave us sandwiches called *muffalettas* made of round Italian bread filled with antipasto and sausage meats. We would sit and eat them staring down at the river, swollen and shiny and taut-looking, as if you could walk on it. By the week after St. Joseph's Day the air was heavy and hypnotic with the buzzing of insects, and there was a lazy levee smell I loved that was a combination of crabgrass and cowturds. In the afternoon we sat and watched the late light on the surface of the river where pieces of sun would bloat and explode back into the sky. Then the crickets would start. The heat would fade a little and the light would crumple over the crabgrass, long thin shadows that etched into darkness, and sometimes Joey said his mother said it was like a Sicilian night.

Food for St. Joseph's Day

SHRIMP-STUFFED ARTICHOKES

Serves 6

6 large artichokes, cleaned and pared
2 lemons, cut in half
1½ pounds shrimp, cooked and cut into bite-size pieces
¾ pound butter, cut into ½-inch pieces
7 cups fresh breadcrumbs
1 large onion, minced
3 cloves garlic, minced
3 cups Parmesan cheese, grated
1 cup flat leaf parsley, minced
1 tablespoon lemon rind, minced

Preheat oven to 350 degrees. Boil artichokes for 15 to 20 minutes until tender and reserve about 2 cups of the boiling liquid. Cool artichokes under cold water. Squeeze halved lemons over artichokes to keep them from turning brown. In a large skillet, sauté the onion and garlic in 4 tablespoons of butter until soft. Add the breadcrumbs and ½ pound additional butter and cook until breadcrumbs are golden.

Add shrimp and lemon rind, and taste the mixture for seasoning. Remove the thistles from the artichokes and begin stuffing by spooning stuffing mixture under each leaf and filling the center cavity. Arrange stuffed artichokes in a casserole, dot with remaining butter, and bake in a 350-degree oven for 20 minutes until butter is melted and artichokes are completely warm.

FLAGEOLETS

Serves 6

1 10-ounce can flageolets
1 4-ounce can tomato paste
1 onion, minced
1 teaspoon oregano
1 teaspoon basil
1 teaspoon thyme
½ teaspoon salt
¼ teaspoon pepper

Drain flageolets, saving the juice. Combine tomato paste, minced onion, oregano, basil, thyme, salt and pepper. Simmer for 45 minutes, adding reserved flageolets juice as needed. Add flageolets and simmer to warm through. Taste for seasoning, adding more salt and pepper if needed. And more flageolet juice if mixture is too dry. Note: Flageolets are very good served with the broiled lamb recipe on page 91.

CRAWFISH ÉTOUFFÉE

Serves 6

5 pounds live crawfish
2 teaspoons brown roux (see page 112)
1 cup scallions, minced
1 cup onions, minced
½ cup celery, chopped
1 clove garlic
2 cups fish stock
2 cups tomatoes, peeled, seeded and chopped

1 tablespoon Worcestershire sauce
1 teaspoon pepper
¼ teaspoon cayenne pepper
2 teaspoons salt
6 cups cooked long-grain rice

Boil crawfish for 5 minutes and remove meat from shells. Warm brown roux in a casserole and add scallions, onions, celery and garlic. Cook for 5 minutes over medium heat. Add fish stock and boil to thicken. Add tomatoes, Worcestershire sauce, cayenne pepper and salt, and simmer for ½ hour. Stir in crawfish and continue cooking to warm. Pour into a bowl and serve with cooked rice.

SPICED STEWED OKRA

Serves 6

½ pound bacon
1¾ cups onion, chopped
1 green pepper, chopped
1½ pounds okra, cleaned and cut crosswise
3 tomatoes peeled, seeded and chopped
2 teaspoons crushed chili pepper
1 teaspoon salt

Fry bacon until crisp. Remove from pan, set bacon aside to drain, and save fat. Add onion and green pepper to fat and cook until soft. Add okra and cook for 15 minutes. Add tomatoes, chili pepper and salt and cook for 10 additional minutes. Serve garnished with bacon.

FISH AND SHELLFISH STEW

Serves 6

4 onions, chopped
1 cup olive oil
2 cans Italian tomatoes, drained and chopped
3 cloves garlic, minced
1 tin anchovies
1 quart clam broth
1 cup white wine
1 teaspoon oregano
1 teaspoon fennel

1 teaspoon basil
½ teaspoon black pepper
½ teaspoon crushed chili pepper
1 cup orzo (tiny pasta)
1 pound fresh scrod
1 pound shrimp
½ pound scallops
1 dozen cherrystone clams, steamed open

In a large pot, sauté onion in ½ cup of olive oil until soft. Add tomatoes. Puree garlic, anchovies and anchovy oil and add to onions. Add clam broth, wine, oregano, fennel, basil, black pepper and chili pepper. Simmer for ½ hour. Add additional ½ cup of olive oil. Bring mixture to a boil. Add orzo and continue boiling for 5 minutes. Add scrod, shrimp and scallops. Reduce heat and simmer for about 8 minutes. Add clams and cook an additional 2 minutes.

COLD LEEKS

Serves 6

6 leeks
Vinaigrette Sauce

Cut leeks to about 7 inches long, discarding the tough upper part. Slit the green parts in half, lengthwise, leaving ½ inch of the root intact. Spread leaves and wash leeks under cold water. Put in casserole, cover with cold water, and bring to a boil. Simmer for 10 minutes. Drain and cool under cold water. Refrigerate for one hour to chill completely. Serve with ½ cup vinaigrette sauce.

Vinaigrette Sauce

Yields ½ cup

1 teaspoon paprika
½ teaspoon Creole mustard or horseradish mustard
2 tablespoons tarragon vinegar
¼ teaspoon cayenne pepper
½ teaspoon salt
7 tablespoons olive oil

Combine paprika, mustard, vinegar, cayenne pepper and salt in a bowl. Slowly dribble in olive oil in a steady stream while beating constantly.

PECAN PRALINES

Makes 2 dozen 2½-inch cookies

2 tablespoons butter
⅓ cup heavy cream
2 cups sugar
⅓ cup brown sugar
½ cup water
dash of salt
1 teaspoon vanilla extract
2¼ cups pecans, chopped

Spread butter on two large baking sheets. Warm the cream. Combine sugar, brown sugar, water and salt in a deep skillet and simmer over low heat for 10 minutes. Add warmed cream, vanilla extract and pecans. Spoon pralines onto cookie sheet and allow to cool.

WHEN I was eleven or twelve I used to go crabbing with a net at the lakefront and then come home and go crawfishing in my own back yard. Somebody in the house could always throw whatever I caught into a pot with some spices and make a meal. There are lots of ways of preparing crustaceans in New Orleans, but the simplest is still best: I like going to one of the funky restaurants at the lakefront for a "cold boil" of crab, crawfish and shrimp — iced, served in their shells — eaten with beer. In New Orleans, you can always spot the locals by their speed at peeling shrimp or picking crabmeat. If you're willing to eat with your hands, try it at home. Tell your family or guests to dress in old clothes — tell them to roll up their sleeves — and put a couple of empty platters on the table as "sewers" for empty shells. If you can't get fresh crawfish, a combination of shrimp and crabs will do fine, but remember that the crabs have to be alive when you cook them and go easy on the spices.

Zatarin's Shrimp and Crab Boil is good used in moderation, though too much of it can make people stop breathing temporarily if they're not familiar with New Orleans food.

Food for a Funky Feast

COLD BOIL FOR SIX

2 lemons
3 gallons water
2 stalks celery with leaves, chopped
4 onions, skins intact
4 cloves garlic
¼ cup mustard seeds
¼ cup coriander seeds
2 tablespoons dill seeds
2 tablespoons whole allspice
5 dried red chili peppers
3 bay leaves
1 dozen blue crabs
3 pounds large shrimp, shell on
6 pounds crawfish, shell on

Combine lemons, water, celery, garlic, onion and spices in a large pot and bring to a boil. Add crawfish.. Reduce heat to low and cover the pot. After 5 minutes, add the crabs and re-cover the pot. Cook crawfish and crabs for 5 minutes and add shrimp. Cook all shellfish a final 5 minutes. Drain immediately and cool the shellfish under cold water. Refrigerate until completely chilled. Serve heaped on cracked ice.

RICE in South Louisiana is grown and eaten with zest. Today's rice farmers flood their fields after harvesting and cultivate crawfish. Some of the best New Orleans dishes, like Crawfish Étouffée, are served on rice, others cooked with it —

but Louisiana cookery pays no attention to the rules the rest of America believes in so fervently. Coast to coast, almost any rice recipe you pick up will tell you in the strictest terms that cooked rice must be "dry, white and fluffy." Forget it.

In New Orleans (as in India and other countries where rice is considered a staple) people would just as soon have it moist, colorful and gummy. Europeans and Asians are often mystified by Americans who go to such trouble to make rice dry and then add gravy; elsewhere the idea is that the flavor should be in the rice, not on it.

I remember one year when I was eleven or so and the Mississippi rose above the levee and had to be sandbagged, then broke through the sandbags and flooded the city. The muddy water in our front yard came up to my chest and before the snakes took to paying house-calls, it was fun just wading around and watching things float by. After the first day, kids my age were confined to the house and for the remainder of the flood people ate what was on the shelves or in the icebox, sometimes swapping fresh ingredients or spices with their immediate neighbors. Rice was the order of the day — rice and whatever you had on hand to cook with it. Maybe for that reason I still think of rice when it rains, and the wetter it gets outside the more possibilities occur to me. Two are worth trying if you're cooking for rice-lovers or if you happen to be eating in a small flood. Dirty Rice, made with chicken giblets and livers, is a wonderful side dish with any fowl. And jambalaya, the Louisiana evolution of paella, is a fine main course.

Food for a Small Flood

DIRTY RICE

Serves 6

½ pound chicken gizzards
½ pound chicken livers

1 green pepper, minced
2 onions, minced
2 cloves garlic, minced
4 stalks celery, minced
½ bunch parsley, minced
3 tablespoons olive oil
½ teaspoon pepper
1 teaspoon salt
2 cups long-grained rice
2 cups chicken stock or chicken consomme

Grind chicken livers, gizzards, green pepper, onion and celery. Sauté in olive oil and simmer for ½ hour. Add rice. Let it brown for a couple of minutes, then add the stock or consommé. Stir, cover and cook for 15 minutes. Remove from heat but leave covered for 15 more minutes prior to serving.

DUCK JAMBALAYA

Serves 6

1 duck, cut into eight pieces
1 teaspoon cayenne pepper
1 teaspoon salt
½ cup flour
2 tablespoons bacon fat
1 cup onions, chopped
1 clove garlic, minced
4 cups chicken stock
2 cups tomatoes, chopped
2 cups uncooked rice
1 cup scallions, minced

Combine flour, salt and cayenne pepper and coat each piece of duck with this mixture. Melt bacon fat and brown duck on all sides and remove to a warm plate. Add onions and garlic to bacon fat and cook until soft. Add chicken stock and tomatoes and scrape the casserole well. Return duck to casserole and simmer for one hour. Add rice, cover pot and cook over low heat, adding more stock if necessary until rice is tender. Add 1 cup of scallions and serve right from the casserole.

SAUSAGE AND EGGPLANT JAMBALAYA

Serves 6

½ pound pepperoni, cut into ½-inch chunks
½ pound boiled beef sausage, cut into ½-inch chunks
2 tablespoons cooking oil or bacon fat
1 clove garlic, chopped
½ cup celery, chopped
½ cup onion, chopped
¼ cup green pepper, chopped
1¼ cups converted (not instant) rice, uncooked
2½ cups water
1 tablespoon salt
½ teaspoon cayenne pepper
2 eggplants, cut into ½-inch cubes

Fry pepperoni and boiled beef sausage in cooking oil or bacon fat in a large casserole. Save 4 tablespoons of this fat. Remove sausages to towel and pat dry. Add garlic, celery, onion and green pepper to fat. Cook over low heat until soft. Add rice and stir. Add water, salt and cayenne pepper and bring mixture to a boil. Add cubed eggplant and cooked sausage. Simmer over low flame for 45 minutes, adding extra water if necessary to avoid sticking or burning.

ANOTHER of my childhood memories connected with food puts oysters together with thinking. How I got to that one, I don't know. A common superstition has oysters as an aphrodisiac, but I've never heard it said that they induced thought. I remember the fun of going to oyster bars in the French Quarter with my father when I was too small to reach up to the bar and he had to hand me down the freshly shucked oysters, one by one. And I recall an overnight trip I took with my mother, downriver on an oyster lugger, to watch the men load barrels of oil onto a dock and pick up barrels of oysters in return. The taste of fresh live oysters in the raw morning, the brackish morning marsh smell of the river where it nears the Delta and the feel of the wet air, warm on your skin, is something you never forget — but it's more connected to burgeoning hedonism than it is to thought.

The closest I can come to oysters-and-thinking is a memory of the walks I took by myself around the docks or along the river levee. By then, the Huey Long administration had had an unpleasant influence on an already politically corrupt city, and though I wasn't yet aware of having been touched by the corruption, I was more afraid of being forced to leave New Orleans than of anything else in my life. I used to walk around and wonder why. Often I would buy an Oyster Poor Boy and take it with me to munch on while I walked.

If you're going for a hike, to be by yourself and think, taking an Oyster Poor Boy with you is not such a bad idea. I wouldn't be dumb enough to recommend it as brain food — but on the other hand . . .

Food for Thought

OYSTER POOR BOY FOR ONE

½ pint shucked oysters
dash of cayenne pepper
dash of black pepper
1 egg
¼ cup evaporated milk
dash of salt
½ cup cornmeal
1 cup fresh breadcrumbs
2 tablespoons melted butter
oil for deep frying
6 inches French bread
½ cup shredded lettuce
4 slices tomato
Creole tartar sauce or hot Louisiana pepper sauce

Pat the oysters dry and season with cayenne and black pepper. Beat egg, evaporated milk and salt until frothy. Roll oysters in cornmeal, dip in egg mixture, and coat with breadcrumbs. Deep-fry the oysters and when they are golden brown, transfer them to paper towels to drain.

Slice the bread lengthwise and pull out the doughy part to create two hollow boatlike shells. Spread with melted butter and toast in 350-degree oven. To assemble Poor Boy, coat the warmed bread with tartar sauce (or hot sauce), stack shredded lettuce, tomato slices and fried oysters and eat at once.

I LEFT New Orleans when I was fifteen.

I went to live in Madrid when I was twenty-one.

The difference between Louisiana under the Long administration and Spain under the Franco regime was not as noticeable as you would think.

3

Spain

LIKE a lot of good American cooks, Lillian is fond of eating Spanish food as long as she doesn't know what it is. If I cook Spanish, I tell her it's French and if I cook Portuguese, I tell her it's mine. The Iberian Peninsula is not famous for its cuisine, and at least in a culinary sense Napoleon was right: Europe ends at the Pyrenees.

Most people make the mistake of thinking that Spanish food is something like Mexican food, which is a big mistake. With few exceptions, Iberian cooking is quite bland in terms of hot seasoning, and spicy Mexican food is anathema to the Spanish palate.

Like Creole cooking, a taste for Iberian food comes more easily to Americans if they have a sense of the place, what it feels like and why the cooking is part of the landscape. Geologically, the Iberian Peninsula is more fragmented than anybody would believe — so rent by ridges and mountain ranges that communication was always difficult. Spain was, is, tribal. No two regions ever agree on anything for long — a Basque doesn't do business with a Castillian any more than a Catalonian sings with an Andalusian — and all of them would rather break bread with a French person than with each other.

Madrid in the '50's was a fun, clumsy city. People from other countries either despised it or loved it — rightly so, as Hemingway said of bullfighting, since any response was reasonable save indifference. At twenty-one, I went to live in Spain for a month and stayed seven years — then went back for another year; then another. There was a time in my life when I couldn't stay away from the place; and I have a sense that the time is coming back.

Among the things I miss is the food.

THE opening sentence of *Don Quixote* refers to an *olla podrida,* or rotten pot, a meal of meats and vegetables boiled together. The dish is still eaten today. In Madrid, it's called a *cocido* and if there were such a thing as a Spanish national dish, this would be it, since every province in the Peninsula has its own version. I have some friends who cook it whenever one of those sleek icy winds comes careening out of the Sierras, and their apartment, high on a hilly cobblestone street in the old part of Madrid, appears to hold the smell of the steaming pot as if the walls had ripened with it; the strength and richness of central Spain are in the odor — full, delicate and deep.

The *Cocido Madrileño* is served in three courses. First comes the broth, with thin noodles floating in it, a good consommé. Second the vegetables: boiled potatoes, chick-peas, carrots, cabbage and onions. Third the meats, usually chunks of beef with port, salt pork, chorizo, morcilla (blood sausage), chicken and sometimes meatballs. The whole thing is served with hot crusty bread and if you liked boiled food, *cocido* is habit-forming.

There's a reason for its popularity throughout the Peninsula apart from taste. The original of the *cocido* is an ancient Jewish dish called *adafina.* During the Spanish Inquisition, the only way you could prove you were Christian was to be seen eating pork in public, since both Jews and Moors shunned pork. The *adafina* had no pork and neither did the *olla podrida,* so the *cocido* — Jewish by birth — became the Spanish national test for Christianity. I have my own version (adding turnips, oxtail and corned beef) which according to Lillian ought to be the Jewish national test for insanity. She refers to it, I'm sorry to say, as Feiblemania, but she usually asks for seconds.

The *cocido* is as simple or as elaborate as you want. Almost any of the meats and vegetables can be withheld without ruining it and the dish stands as a good way to combat the cold in any country. In certain parts of Spain, at the end of the *cocido,* people mash small crusts of bread into the leftover meat and eat them. This process is called a *pringada,* the infinitive is *pringar* and the taste is obscene. It's good enough to dump today's trendy health rules long enough to try.

The trick in cooking any boiled meal is to keep the vegetables from getting mushy. I use carrots at the beginning to flavor the broth, take them out toward the end, and put in fresh ones for eating.

Food for Winter

COCIDO MADRILEÑO
(Boiled Chicken and Vegetables)

Serves 6 to 10

1 cup dried chick-peas
6 pounds stewing fowl
2 pounds beef brisket
1 pound smoked ham, cut into 1-inch slices
½ pound salt pork, cut into 1-inch slices
1 onion, minced
3 carrots, peeled and cut in half
3 leeks, cleaned and cut in half
1 head garlic, unpeeled
1 bay leaf
6 sprigs parsley

1 teaspoon black pepper
6 links chorizo
2 pounds cabbage, cut into 2-inch wedges
8 small potatoes

Soak chick-peas in water overnight and drain. Place chick-peas, stewing fowl and brisket in a large (12-quart) casserole with 5½ quarts of cold water. Bring to a boil and reduce heat. Simmer for 1½ hours. Skim off foam. Add smoked ham, salt pork, onion, carrots, leeks, garlic, bay leaf, parsley and pepper. Simmer for 30 minutes. Prick chorizos and place in skillet. Cover with water and boil for 5 minutes. Drain. Add chorizo, cabbage and potatoes to casserole. Simmer for 30 minutes. Mash the head of garlic against the side of the pot with the back of wooden spoon and discard the outside. Adjust seasoning, adding additional salt and pepper if necessary, and serve.

One of the things I learned from the *cocido* is that beef and chicken are good boiled together, which permits me to stick to my rule of avoiding water: short ribs boiled in chicken broth (fresh or canned) with tomatoes and vegetables make a fine soup and a good main course.

FEIBLEMANIA

Serves 10

½ pound salt pork, cut into ¼-inch cubes
2 oxtails
1 pound corned beef
1 pound brisket of beef
1 small chicken
½ pound pork, cut into ½-inch cubes
1 head garlic, unpeeled
3 onions, quartered
6 stalks celery, cut in half
3 turnips, pared and quartered
12 small potatoes
6 carrots, peeled and quartered
2 bay leaves
1 bunch parsley
1 tablespoon black peppercorns
1 cabbage, quartered
1 teaspoon saffron (optional)

2 cups green beans
1 can chick-peas, drained
chicken broth

Fry salt pork in a large casserole over medium heat. When golden, add oxtails and brown on all sides. Add corned beef and beef brisket, cover with cold chicken stock, and bring to a simmer. Simmer for 2 hours. Add chicken, pork cubes, garlic, onions, celery, turnips, potatoes, carrots, bay leaves, parsley, peppercorns, cabbage and saffron if desired. Add more cold chicken stock to cover and simmer for one hour. Add green beans and chick-peas. Simmer for 15 more minutes and serve.

DURING the '50's before I was able to make my living writing, I worked at any job I could get. I had no work permit, so I had to pretend to be Spanish or be out of a job. For those years I walked around Madrid with all kinds of Spaniards (almost anybody who didn't speak English), and formed certain food habits that have stayed with me for life.

In the evening in Madrid it is the custom to walk from bar to bar with friends and have a glass of wine with a small dish of whatever *tapa* (appetizer) is the specialty of that bar. Each place boasts its own *tapa*, from the low-down bars that only serve one, to the posh places that have an assortment of forty or fifty. The custom of bar-walking is called a *chateo*, from the shape of the small wine glasses (*chato* means snub-nosed). Lillian likes a *chateo* better than sitting in the best bar in Europe. The smell of the simmering *tapas* rolling out onto the street, tinged with the scent of sawdust and old wine, keeps you hungry for hours, and you develop a taste for favorites: I like veal kidneys grilled with lemon juice and parsley and garlic; tripe *à la Madrileña* in tomato sauce cooked with chorizo, ham, sausage, onions, garlic, carrots, paprika, white wine, leeks and cloves; shrimp or langostinos thrown on a hot griddle in their shells with nothing but coarse salt; mushroom caps grilled alone or skewered with bits of ham; tiny fowl the size of hummingbirds fried crisp; fried squid; stewed octopus, boiled crab — and so on. Because Madrid is the center of Spain, fresh food and seafood from all the provinces come in daily, via roads that lead into the city like spokes of a wheel. Many *tapas* make a good main course. Three or more can make a banquet.

Food for Tapas

FAVA BEANS WITH SAUSAGE AND MINT

Serves 6

1 pound chorizo
1 tablespoon lard
¼ pound salt pork, cut in a fine dice
½ cup scallions, minced
1 clove garlic, minced
½ cup white wine
½ cup water
1 tablespoon mint
1 bay leaf
½ teaspoon salt
½ teaspoon pepper
4 cups fava beans, cooked

Prick sausages with a fork and blanch for 5 minutes in boiling water. Drain and slice sausages into ¼-inch slices. Melt lard and cook salt pork until golden. Transfer the crisp salt pork to a paper towel to drain. Add scallions and garlic to fat in the pan and cook until soft but not brown. Add wine, water, pork crisps, mint, bay leaf, salt and pepper. Bring to a boil and then simmer for 20 minutes. Add the beans and cook until heated through.

GRILLED SHRIMP

Serves 6

1½ cups olive oil
2 tablespoons lemon juice
1 clove garlic, minced
2 tablespoons chili pepper

2 tablespoons cayenne pepper
3 tablespoons coarse ground black pepper
2 pounds unshelled jumbo shrimp
lemon wedges

Combine olive oil, lemon juice, garlic, chili pepper, cayenne and black pepper. Add shrimp and marinate for 2 hours. Grill shrimp with shell on and serve immediately with lemon wedges.

GRILLED KIDNEYS

Serves 6

¼ cup Worcestershire sauce
½ cup lemon juice
2 cloves garlic, minced
1 teaspoon salt
½ teaspoon pepper
2 pounds veal kidneys, split lengthwise in half, trimmed of all fat and cut into 1-inch cubes
1 bunch chives, chopped

Combine Worcestershire sauce, lemon, garlic, salt and pepper in a shaker. Allow mixture to steep overnight.

Lightly oil a griddle. Allow griddle to get very hot. Fry kidneys, shaking sauce mixture over them as they cook. Garnish with minced chives and serve.

SALT COD WITH TOMATOES, ONIONS AND GARLIC

Serves 6

2 pounds salt cod, shredded and soaked in cold water 24 hours
1 cup olive oil
2 onions, minced
3 cups tomatoes, chopped
4 cloves garlic, minced
¼ teaspoon black pepper

Heat ½ cup olive oil in a large skillet. Drain salt cod and rinse under cold water and pat dry. Stir in cod and one-half of the onion and cook for 5 minutes. Reduce heat to low and cook for 30 minutes until most of the liquid has evaporated. In a separate pan, heat remaining olive oil, add garlic and onions and cook until soft. Add tomatoes and stir mixture to mash. Add tomato mixture to cod and simmer together for 5 minutes.

TRIPE STEW WITH VEAL, HAM, CHICKEN AND SAUSAGES

Serves 6

1 pound veal shank
1½ pounds tripe, cut in cubes
2 teaspoons salt
1 cup navy beans
½ pound smoked pork sausage
¼ pound lean smoked ham
1 2-pound chicken, cut into eighths
2 carrots
1 large onion, peeled and cut
3 tablespoons lard
1 cup onion, chopped
1 teaspoon cumin
1 bay leaf
½ cup parsley

Put veal, tripe and salt in a 5-quart pan. Cover with water and boil. Simmer for 2 hours. Cook and drain beans. Put sausages in skillet. Prick with knife. Cover with water and bring to boil. Simmer for 5 minutes. Drain and dry. Put ham, sausages and chicken in a 4-quart pan. Cover with water. Boil. Simmer for 15 minutes. Skim off foam. Add carrots, onions and simmer 15 minutes more. Take meat from bird and cube. Slice up sausages. Set vegetables, meat and broth aside. Drain tripe and veal. Cut the veal into small bite-size pieces. In a 6-quart casserole add lard, onions, pepper, cumin. Cook 5 minutes. Add tripe, veal, chicken, ham, carrots, sliced onion, bay leaf, and parsley. Add 3 cups broth. Simmer 10 minutes. Taste for seasoning and serve.

OLD and New Castile, named for the castles built for protection against the Moors, occupy the great granite plateau in the middle of Spain, the center of which is Madrid. Meats are grilled outdoors in the countryside of the central plateau over coals that have been topped with fresh branches of rosemary or thyme, the smoke from the burning herbs permeating the food. Mountain trout is cooked that way here, sizzled whole in a skillet that's been rubbed with *serrano* (mountain-cured) ham, and thin slices of the ham are also placed inside the fish.

In La Mancha, Don Quixote's province of Old Castile, a fine vegetable dish called *Pisto Mancheqo* is simmered to a puree containing tomatoes, green peppers, zucchini, onions and (sometimes) garlic.

Food for Vegetarians

PISTO

¼ cup olive oil
3 medium onions
2 sweet green or red peppers, chopped
1½ pounds zucchini, chopped
1 eggplant, peeled and chopped
1 32-ounce can tomatoes
4–6 cloves garlic
salt and pepper
1 teaspoon sugar

In ¼ cup olive oil (or olive and Wesson mixed) briefly fry chopped onion, then add the green peppers, zucchini, eggplant and tomatoes with liquid. Cook over low flame for 30 minutes, then add chopped garlic, salt, pepper, sugar. Cook about 15 minutes more. (The whole dish shouldn't take more than an hour or so.) If served hot, put grated cheese (provolone, mozzarella, Monterey jack, etc.) on top.

ANDALUSIA, the southern part of the Peninsula, is made up of eight provinces named by the Moors "Al Andalus" — a place of "sensuality and repose" — and inhabited by them for eight centuries. It is as different from the starkness of the Castiles as South Louisiana is from New England.

Andalusia is the hedonistic Spain that has been romanticized to death by composers, lyricists, writers and other low-life. Down through the years, foreigners have written about the region with relentless energy, missing the point nearly every time. The Carmen of Merimée or Bizet is about as Spanish as the *gazpacho* served in Paris.

I went looking one October and found thirty-three different recipes for *gazpacho* between Cadiz and Granada. Basically, *gazpacho* is a cold soup containing tomatoes, oil and often vinegar, garlic, the crustless dough of white bread, water, a great many vegetables and sometimes fruits or nuts, from white floating grapes to crushed almonds to cherries. The ways of making it are countless and it has been around a long time. The word *gazpacho* comes from an Arabic term for "soaked bread," the dish is mentioned in Greek and Roman literature as a "potable food" and there are references to it in both testaments of the Bible.

Up to the middle of this century *gazpacho* was made with a mortar and pestle. I happened by accident to be in Seville the summer the first electric blender appeared from America, some thirty years ago. For one suspicious month the whole town ignored it — then, slowly, it caught on. By mid-June, Cadillacs and Buicks no longer impressed people so much, and by July the American electric razor fell by the wayside. No status symbol has ever quite achieved the posture of the American electric blender in Andalusia. The people of Seville kept them like fine china, in locked cases on velvet, and from then on nobody who was anybody made *gazpacho* in a mortar and pestle.

When Christopher Columbus, who is buried in the Seville Cathedral, left on his first voyage, he sailed out of the Guadalquivir River, and it is known that he brought back to Seville many curious objects from the New World. I was sitting in the Seville library one day, doing some research on Columbus with the window open, and I couldn't hear the castanets for the blenders.

As a twenty-one-year-old American, I felt responsible for bringing back to Spain the Old Ways of doing things, and I went on making *gazpacho* with a mortar and pestle for ten years before I figured the hell with it. Now I make it in a blender and I make it every summer. Over a period of ten years, *gazpacho* has been the first thing Lillian asks for on the Vineyard when the heat starts. She says I am the only person who makes it right, which is what any Southern Belle says when she doesn't want to make something herself.

There is only one trick to *gazpacho* beyond choosing the recipe you like best. When you serve it, chop up or dice every raw vegetable you can find that has a crunchy texture, put them all out in separate small dishes and let people sprinkle them on top as they would condiments. This usually requires peeling several onions, so remember that the fastest way to peel an onion is to slice it in half crosswise first. For those who like fruit floating on *gazpacho* (I happen not to), add a dish of pitted fresh cherries and one of sliced grapes. Chop up a few hard-boiled eggs too, and put them in a dish. Properly served, *gazpacho* should have the look of a multicolored summer jubilee, with each person decorating his or her bowl according to taste from the line of dishes. If you have a turntable, use that; if you don't, pass the dishes from person to person. Do this slowly and deliberately, and don't make the mistake of thinking it's boring — it isn't. Most people like to play with food as infants do, and adults don't often get the chance.

Of the recipes I've collected, I like these two best:

Food for Thirst

GAZPACHO I

Serves 6

2 medium-size cucumbers, peeled and chopped
5 medium-size tomatoes, peeled and chopped
1 onion, chopped
1 green pepper, coarsely chopped
1 red pepper, coarsely chopped
2 cloves garlic
4 cups French bread, crusts removed
4 cups tomato juice
¼ cup red wine vinegar
4 tablespoons olive oil

Puree cucumbers, tomatoes, onion, peppers, garlic, bread, vinegar and tomato juice in a blender until smooth. Pour puree into a bowl, whisk in olive oil, and chill thoroughly before serving. Garnish with croutons and additional minced fresh vegetables. Note: If you like a richer soup and are not averse to cheating, add a dollop of sour cream.

GAZPACHO II

Serves 6

1 medium-size cucumber, chopped
3 medium-size tomatoes, peeled and chopped
½ onion, chopped
1 red pepper, chopped
2 cloves garlic
4 cups French bread, crusts removed
1 fresh chili pepper, chopped
¼ cup fresh coriander, chopped
4 cups tomato juice
¼ cup sherry vinegar
1 cucumber, peeled, seeded and sliced thin
2 tomatoes, peeled, seeded and chopped fine

½ onion, minced
1 red pepper, minced
1 green pepper, minced
4 tablespoons oilive oil
salt

Puree coarsely chopped cucumbers, tomatoes, onion, red pepper with garlic, French bread, fresh chili pepper, coriander, tomato juice and vinegar in a blender until smooth. Pour puree into a large bowl. Whisk in olive oil and stir in finely minced cucumber, tomato, onion, red and green pepper. Adjust seasoning with salt and chill completely before serving.

ANDALUSIA is known in Spain as the "zone of frying." What they fry is fish and they do it better than anybody. From *chanquetes* (no bigger than minnows, fried whole like whitebait) to *boquerones* (fresh anchovies fried with their tails squeezed together like infinitesimal fish bouquets) to squid — and on to larger species — fish is cooked with a lightness that seems magic. I once saw a married couple strolling in Seville's Calle Sierpes, the women carrying a parasol to keep the sun off her person and a cone of fried fish to keep her husband on it.

What the Andalusians know that nobody else seems to is how to deep-fry, in very hot oil, without the temperature of the oil going down every time you put a cold fish in it. The problem is a little bit like boiling several ears of corn together without ever causing the water to drop below the boiling point. I watched a street-cook in Cadiz fry fish outdoors one day for an hour, wondering what his secret was, till I realized that he didn't have an icebox. The reason the temperature of hot oil is lowered by a cold fish is that the fish is cold. His weren't. They were lying on a slab of marble next to him with the sun on them and they were already warm when he cooked them. Americans are so scared of infection that we tend to be as antiseptic in our cooking as we are in our thinking. When we fry food, it usually goes straight from the icebox into the oil, pausing only long enough to be floured or breaded. Try allowing it to become room-temperature first and see what happens. Fish can't spoil in those few minutes, and the lightness of the resulting fry is worth the extra step. The same is true, incidentally, for any other fried food, including Southern fried chicken. I once phoned Lillian from Seville to report this, and she sighed. "Honey," she said, "if you're calling from Andalusia to tell me that, you can't afford to eat fried fish. Now sober up and come home." Frying was one of the things we never could agree about.

Most Spanish food is used as a form of communication, and every cook has his own way of preparing it, region to region, district to district, house to house. Some of the Andalusian dishes I like best are as follows:

Food for Fun

FRIED SQUID

Serves 6

3 pounds fresh squid, cleaned in ice water
3 eggs, more as needed
½ cup milk, more as needed
6 cups garlic breadcrumbs, more as needed
6 cups good olive oil, more as needed

Boil squid for 1 hour and 10 minutes in plenty of well-salted water. Drain and cool under cold water. Cut squid into ½-inch rings. Combine eggs and milk. Soak squid rings in this mixture and then dip each piece in breadcrumbs to coat. Set up a deep-fryer with 6 cups of olive oil. When oil is hot enough to cause breadcrumbs to sizzle, fry squid in small batches to avoid sticking and to allow each ring to cook until crisp and golden. Serve heaped on a platter.

SAUTÉED VEAL WITH SHERRY AND GREEN OLIVES

Serves 6

1 cup olive oil
2 cups onions, minced
1 tablespoon garlic, minced
2 green peppers, minced
2 cups mushrooms, sliced
5 tomatoes, peeled, seeded and chopped
12 green olives, pitted
½ cup serrano ham, finely chopped
2 tablespoons almonds, ground
6 veal scallops
salt and pepper
1 cup flour
½ cup sherry
½ cup water

Heat ½ cup olive oil in a big skillet. Add the onions, garlic and green pepper and cook until soft. Add the mushrooms, tomatoes, olives, ham and ground almonds and bring mixture to a boil. Season veal scallops with salt and pepper and lightly dust with flour. Heat remaining olive oil and sauté the veal until golden on each side. Transfer veal to a platter. Discard any olive oil remaining in sauté pan and deglaze with water and sherry. Add tomato sauce and stir well. Add veal to sauce and warm together until heated through.

ANISE AND SESAME SEED COOKIES

12 cookies

1 cup olive oil
1 strip lemon peel, 2 inches long and ½ inch wide
2 teaspoons anise seeds
2 teaspoons sesame seeds
½ cup dry white wine
1 teaspoon lemon rind, minced

1 teaspoon orange rind, minced
⅓ cup sugar
2¼ cups all-purpose flour
1 tablespoon ground cinnamon
¼ cup sliced almonds

Heat olive oil. Add lemon peel, anise and sesame seeds and remove from heat to cool to room temperature. Discard lemon peel and pour the oil, sesame seeds and anise seeds into a large mixing bowl. Stir in wine, lemon rind, orange rind and sugar and mix until sugar dissolves. Sift flour and cinnamon into oil and wine mixture a little at a time, stirring well between each addition. Let dough rest for 30 minutes. Preheat oven to 400 degrees. Divide dough into 12 pieces and shape each into a flat cookie. Place cookies 2 inches apart on an ungreased baking sheet and press 6 almond slices into the top of each cookie. Bake in 400-degree oven for 40 minutes until cookies are firm to the touch.

ALONG the southern coast not far from the city of Cadiz is a small fishing village called Sanlúcar de Barrameda, where they sometimes eat red beans with rice, much as people do in New Orleans. But Andalusian country folk often follow a bean dish with a small piece of charcoal from the stove and wash it down with water. (Charcoal absorbs intestinal gas.) This practice is not limited to Spain: any American drugstore will sell you charcoal capsules. I recommend them. Kidney beans of all kinds have the same effect, and eating them at dinner means you run the risk of farting the national anthem before midnight.

In the early '60's I lived in Sanlúcar for almost a year, working on the beginning of a novel that was to be written ten years later in Lillian's house and published as *The Columbus Tree;* I stayed in the Medina Sidonia palace at the very top of the village, overlooking the place where the brownish water of the Guadalquivir River pours into the green of the open sea. The palace is owned by a woman named Luisa Isabel Alvarez de Toledo, Duchess of Medina Sidonia, whose family archives, kept in the palace attic, date back to the eleventh century.

Floor to ceiling, wall to wall, the attic consisted of two large rooms full of uncollated papers — some of them roughly collected by century — others just stacked. The duchess was afraid of allowing people into the archives, since many visitors stole papers, and Franco himself had offered to have the archives collated "at no expense." Despite his power as a dictator, Generalissimo Francisco Franco curried favor with the nobility in an almost craven way, and when he gained control over private archives, he censored them. Silly as it seems, he liked to whitewash history in an attempt to clean up the Inquisition and minimize the expulsion of the Moors and Jews from Spain. The duchess was vehemently against Franco as well as everything he stood for, and I was too, so she enlisted my help.

Working with the underground was easy for me because there wasn't much I could do past picking people up at an airport at night, delivering them to their destinations or helping to get them out of the country. Helping collate the archives presented more of a challenge.

One day I found an early-fifteenth-century letter from a female cousin, a countess of the Medina Sidonia family, addressed to the then duchess, saying she had taken a five-day carriage ride from Sanlúcar to Seville (a couple of hours by car today) which was uncomfortable and unrewarding except for a great new recipe her cook had come up with. The letter was dated in December and the weather, the countess said, was unusually cold. Her cook, it seems, had a friend who had taught him to boil meat with nothing but a bay leaf, salt and two rams' horns for hours until nothing was left of the meat but a thick dark sticky substance. The cook put the substance outside till it was cold and hard, then cut it into cubes with a knife. During her trip to Seville, the countess said, she was forced to stop at several inns, and in one of them her cook went to work with the cubes he had made. All he asked for was a cup of boiling water. At this point the countess begged her cousin to believe what she was about to recount, swearing on her mother's grave that it was true: her cook dropped one of the cubes into the cup of boiling water. Pretty soon, the countess said, the cube melted and the water turned into beef broth. She was never so surprised. At first she was too suspicious to taste the broth, but her cook persuaded her. She knew that no one was going to believe her, but the broth was not bad. Evidently all you needed was a pair of rams' horns and you could make a broth of anything and travel with it. The countess did not recommend it to the duchess for *home* use, but she said it was better than the disgusting food you got when you traveled. "Anything," she concluded, "is better than the food served at an inn."

A few years later, I was traveling on the Concorde with Lillian from New York to London when she opened a slouch bag and took out something large wrapped in foil. "It's plain broiled chicken with tarragon on it," she said, "but it's better than the vile stuff they serve on planes. Anything's better than airplane food."

The recipe of the fifteenth-century Medina Sidonia countess for bouillon cubes is a little tricky to make due to the shortage of rams' horns, but here are a couple of Lillian's ideas for travel food that are very good.

Food for Travel

TARRAGON CHICKEN

Serves 2

1 small roasting chicken
2 tablespoons butter
1 lemon, cut in half
2 tablespoons dried tarragon or 4 tablespoons fresh tarragon
¼ cup lemon juice
1 tablespoon salt
2 teaspoons black pepper

Preheat oven to 350 degrees. Tuck 1 tablespoon butter between the skin and meat of each chicken breast. Season cavity with salt, pepper and sprinkling of tarragon and stuff with cut lemon. Truss the bird. Moisten skin with lemon juice, season with remaining salt, pepper and tarragon. Roast chicken in 350-degree oven for about 20 minutes per pound. Cool completely. Refrigerate and serve sliced.

TARTAR STEAK

Serves 6

2 pounds top sirloin with all fat removed
2 egg yolks
¼ cup Bermuda onion, minced
¼ cup capers, minced
2 tablespoons anchovy, minced
dash of olive oil
dash of Tabasco sauce
1 clove garlic, minced (optional)
salt and pepper to taste

Grind sirloin. Mix in egg yolks, onion, capers, anchovy, olive oil, Tabasco sauce and garlic, if desired. Season with salt and pepper to taste. Serve very cold with slices of pumpernickel bread.

The second recipe is one I filched from Lillian and then altered. Eaten on crackers, it's good with drinks on any flight — and please let's call it Tartar Steak, not *Steak Tartare.* For some reason, expensive American restaurants think it's spiffy to say things in French. A startling percentage of the American public has picked up this habit, in the old American belief that proper etiquette is to do what the waiters do, and the result is that plain American speech is getting sprinkled with French phrases almost to the degree that Russian was in the nineteenth century. A headwaiter is no longer a headwaiter, he's a "maître d' "; pure gravy isn't pure gravy, it's "au jus"; a fish called turbot is pronounced "tur-bow," and Tartar Steak (so called because the Tartars carried meat under their saddles or saddlebags) is called "*Steak Tartare.*" Let's knock it off.

Of all the dishes in Spain, the most famous and the most messed with is something called *paella.* Lillian used to wince at the sight of *paella* till I made it for her outdoors at a picnic one day, and then she got so interested in the cooking that she forgot what she was eating and wound up liking it.

If fifty recipes for *gazpacho* are easy to come by, multiply that by ten for *paella* and you'll be missing some, since all it has to contain is rice, saffron and whatever looks cheap and fresh at the market. The dish is named after the *paellera,* the pan in which it's made, but an iron skillet will do just as well. If you like cooking outdoors, a *paella* can turn a picnic into a party.

The original dish came from a freshwater lagoon known as La Albufera, close to the city of Valencia on Spain's Levantine coast; it contained eels, green beans and snails and was eaten with small whole onions instead of bread. The dish you see on restaurant menus all over the world listed as *Paella Valenciana* is probably a concoction, and certainly a misnomer. Among the vast spectrum of *paellas,* the Valencian one is not high on the scale, for the Valencians, culinarily speaking, are a tightassed lot, given to rigid inhibitions about the mixing of meat and fish, fish and shellfish and meat with certain other meat. The polychromatic, dramatic-looking dish most people think of as *paella* is to be found around Alicante, and is worth the trouble you have to go through to find it.

The reason *paella* is easier to cook outdoors than indoors has to do with heat control: the pan is large and the flame on a stovetop is usually too limited in area. An electric stove can sometimes do the job if you like electric stoves (I don't) or if you're stuck with one, as Lillian is on the Vineyard. If you're cooking indoors and worst comes to worst, which it often does, you can always put the *paella* into the oven when you're ready to cook the rice.

What you want to do first is prepare things so that you can reach for them when you need them. Take some mussels, clams, shrimp and whitefish (or any combination thereof), and boil all of it in water for the required time — then remove it, save the water and peel the shrimp. Put the shrimp shells back into the same water and boil them for at least 30 minutes or longer. Then take the shells out, discard them and set that water aside.

Let's assume you're outdoors. If you have a barbecue handy, use it. If you don't, use three stones to hold the pan up, then make a fire of wood sticks around them. The sticks should all point inward like spokes, up toward a central point where the fire will be hottest. Light it and wait. When it gets going, place the pan on top and splash a little olive oil into it.

As soon as the oil starts to smoke, add some chicken parts, giblets, pieces of pork and slices of sausage (exact amounts are given below). By now the fire ought to be licking at the entire surface of the bottom of the pan. When the meat is browned on all sides, lift it out, set it aside and replace it with thinly sliced onion. When the onion looks as if it had started to rust, add mashed garlic, tomatoes and (optionally) coarse salt.

What you now have is called a *sofrito.* Mush it all up together with a wooden spoon, take the pan off the flame for long enough to add some paprika, stir it again and put the pan back on. Add some crushed saffron, stir once more and put the meats back into the *sofrito.*

Stir all hell out of that.

About now you ought to check your fire. If it's low, push the partly burned sticks toward the center till the flames are high again.

Then add the rice.

At this point, if people don't gravitate toward the pan, attracted by the smell, you're doing something wrong. The odor should be aromatic, a combination of sea- and land-food, zesty and sharp, the kind of smell that has an immediate effect on the salivary glands and (from time to time) the gonads. Do not answer questions about what you're doing. Let people stand around, and keep doing it. See that somebody gives them a drink while you go on stirring for a couple of minutes until the rice has browned in the *sofrito.*

Now add the water you saved from the seafood and shrimp shells. It should be whitish, and you want twice as much water as rice. Fresh garden peas, squid rings and small artichokes can go in now if you happen to have any hanging around. One last stir, then kill the flames by pulling the last of the wood sticks out of the spoke formation — away from the pan — so that the pan sits on the hot embers. (If you're on a barbecue grill, mash the coals into one flat layer and lower the pan. If you're indoors, good luck.)

The rice is cooked, they say in Alicante, when the rice is cooked. What they mean is, look at it and taste it. Depending on what kind of rice you're using, after about 18 minutes it should be dark yellow and it should have risen almost to the top and sides of the pan. Chew a couple of grains. It shouldn't be too hard or too soft. When it's done, slide the last of the coals out from under the pan with a stick.

This is the time to insert the cooked clams, shrimp, mussels and whitefish — plus any other shellfish you've boiled, lobster or crawfish. You may garnish the finished *paella* with pimiento strips crisscrossed over the top, and you are now finished cooking. Wash your hands.

If you want to eat the *paella* the way they do at an Alicante outdoor family picnic, you and your friends will all be eating out of the pan you cooked in. It goes like this:

First, let people look at it. Seat them in a circle around the pan and give them each a spoon and a fork. Small wooden spoons are best, but any spoons will do. For every couple of people, set out a dish to be used as a sewer for shells and bones.

Next, take a small white plate and place it, upside down, in the very center of the *paella*, on top of the rice.

Now listen carefully. On top of that plate, place another plate, right side up. The second plate should contain a salad composed of lettuce, tomato and onions, with a plain oil and vinegar dressing.

Tell people to use their spoons and tell them to eat the *paella* up to the plate, stopping to pick up their forks and spear a piece of tomato or onion when they want from the salad at the center. By the time the salad is finished, the *paella* around it should be gone too.

Then lift both plates off and expose the final center portion, still warm, for anybody who wants seconds.

You should have a good time at your picnic. If you do, as Lillian says, do not thank me. Pay me.

Food for a Friendly Picnic

PAELLA INGREDIENTS

Serves 6

1 2-pound lobster
6 shrimps, shell on
6 littleneck clams
6 mussels
3 links chorizo
1 small chicken, cut into 12 pieces
2 teaspoons salt
1 teaspoon black pepper
½ cup olive oil
2 ounces pork, cut into ¼-inch cubes
½ cup onions, minced
1 teaspoon garlic, minced
1 red or green pepper, julienned
1 tomato, peeled, seeded and chopped
3 cups long-grain rice, uncooked
¼ teaspoon saffron threads, pulverized
6 cups boiling water
½ cup green peas
2 lemons, cut into 6 wedges

SALAD FOR PAELLA

Serves 6

2 tablespoons vinegar
1 teaspoon salt
6 tablespoons oil
6 tomatoes, cut in wedges
1 head iceberg lettuce, coarsely chopped

Dissolve salt in vinegar and slowly whisk in oil. Toss tomatoes and lettuce with this sauce and serve.

ON the way out of Spain I might as well add this. A Spanish omelet is not what every other country thinks of as a Spanish omelet, Mexico included. What the Mexicans call a Spanish omelet is what the Spanish call a Mexican omelet: everybody blames this mess on everybody else. Lillian calls it a "drek omelet." It usually has a watery tomato sauce with limp-looking onions and pellucid green peppers, and it probably came from Texas.

A real Spanish omelet, served all over the Peninsula, is just a thick potato omelet, sometimes made with sliced onions and sometimes not. You wouldn't catch a tomato or a green pepper anywhere near it and it's good hot or at room temperature. Considering its thickness, the big trick is to flip the omelet over in the skillet while you're making it, which the Spanish do by clapping a dinner plate on top, turning the whole thing upside down in the plate, then sliding the omelet back into the pan. Try that sometime. If you can pull it off, the result is a fine thing to pack in a picnic basket, especially if you're going on a long drive. I took one in the car once when Lillian and I drove from New York to the Vineyard, and along the way she cut it into wedges like a pie. We stopped and ate it by the side of the road, with a couple of bottles of beer, and the taste was so good I promised her I would never made her eat at a fast-food diner again unless we were starving.

Food for the Car

POTATO AND ONION OMELET

Serves 4

2 pounds potatoes, peeled and sliced
1¼ cups olive oil
½ cup chopped onion
4 eggs
1½ teaspoons salt

In a well-oiled skillet, brown the potatoes in the olive oil. Add the chopped onion and cook until soft. Remove from heat and drain off excess oil. In a bowl, beat together the eggs and salt until frothy. Add the onion and potato mixture and continue cooking over medium heat for 6 or 7 minutes. Flip the omelet over and cook for an additional 5 minutes or until solid.

Elsewhere

LATE in the '50's I published my first novel, left Spain and went back to live in New York for a while, hoping it would feel like home. It didn't.

One of the things I was hungry for was other writers, and one of the people I got to know was Santha Rama Rau, who wrote a lot for *The New Yorker.* Santha was kind and generous to new authors, and she said she'd invite four or five people to dinner for me and asked whom I wanted.

Whom I wanted was Lillian Hellman. I hadn't seen her in a long time, and I was twenty-eight now and thought of myself as deeply middle-aged.

I don't remember much about that night except for Lillian's face and what the food was. Santha is a great Indian cook and the meal was hot enough to fuse what might otherwise have been an awkward time.

Food for Curried People

BIRYANI

Serves 6

3 cloves garlic
2 onions, chopped
1½ inch fresh ginger root, peeled and chopped

½ teaspoon ground cumin
½ teaspoon ground coriander seeds
¼ teaspoon mace
¼ teaspoon nutmeg
¼ teaspoon cardamom seeds
¼ teaspoon cinnamon
5 cloves
10 black peppercorns
2 teaspoons salt
2 tablespoons lemon juice
½ cup yogurt
2 tablespoons heavy cream
1 onion, sliced thin
2 tablespoons butter
2 tablespoons oil
2 pheasants, skinned and quartered
1 cup long-grain rice (preferably Basmati rice)
1 teaspoon saffron
2 tablespoons milk
almonds, pistachios, raisins and thin, fried onion rings for garnish

This is a very grand rice dish developed in the palace kitchens of the Moghul emperors. It can be made with lamb or chicken but Santha says that it tastes best with game bird.

First make the marinade by pureeing garlic, chopped onions, fresh ginger root, cumin, coriander, mace, nutmeg, cardamom seeds, cinnamon, cloves, peppercorns, salt and lemon juice in a blender or food processor until it becomes a smooth paste. Put this in a large bowl and add yogurt and heavy cream. Fry the sliced onion in the butter and vegetable oil until golden. Save the butter and oil and mix the onions with the marinade. Pierce the pheasant meat all over with a fork and mix the pheasant with the marinade. Marinate overnight in the icebox.

Next day simmer the marinade and pheasant for 15–20 minutes. In a separate pot, parboil 1 cup of rice with 2 cups of water for 5 minutes (rice will continue to cook when dish is assembled and baked). Soak 1 teaspoon of saffron in 2 tablespoons of milk for 10 minutes.

Take a large casserole and brush with a little of the reserved butter and oil mixture. Put a layer of rice on the bottom of the casserole, then some pieces of meat, spooning marinade lightly over the meat. Continue layering the rice and pheasant until they are used up (there will be marinade left over). Use the handle of a wooden spoon to make holes in the rice-meat mixture and pour the saffron/milk mixture into these holes. Drizzle the reserved oil and butter over the casserole and cover with foil and a tightly fitting lid. Bake in a 300-degree oven for one hour.

The pot should be opened at the table, where guests get the first fragrance of the saffron as the lid and foil are taken off. Biryani should be garnished with raisins and almonds or pistachios fried in butter and some thin-sliced, crisp-fried onion rings.

JHINGA PATIA

Serves 8

4 pounds jumbo shrimp, cleaned
½ cup lemon juice
½ cup cider vinegar
2 teaspoons ground cumin
1 teaspoon turmeric
1 teaspoon hot red pepper
1 teaspoon black pepper
6 teaspoons salt
2 teaspoons black mustard seeds
4 tablespoons ginger root, peeled and chopped fine
2 tablespoons garlic, minced
2 cups onion, chopped
4 cups tomatoes, peeled, seeded and chopped
¼ cup brown sugar
1 tablespoon molasses
⅓ cup coriander leaves, minced
¼ cup fresh chili peppers, chopped
½ cup vegetable oil

Combine the lemon juice, vinegar, cumin, turmeric, red and black pepper and 4 teaspoons salt and mix well. Marinate the shrimp in this mixture at room temperature for ½ hour. Heat vegetable oil in a heavy skillet. Stir in the mustard seeds, remaining 2 teaspoons of salt, the garlic and onions, and cook until the onions are soft and brown. Drain the marinade from the shrimp into the skillet, add the tomatoes and stir for several minutes. Add the brown sugar, molasses and coriander. Drop in the shrimp, turning them in the sauce until they are well coated. Sprinkle fresh chilis, cover the skillet, and continue cooking over medium heat until the shrimp are pink. Serve with boiled rice.

After dinner, Lillian got up to leave and said to me, "You look like both your parents," in a voice that sounded as if she didn't necessarily mean that as a compliment.

Santha went to the door with her and Lillian turned back once and looked hard into the room. She was wearing a veil tight around her face with her head high, her body straight and the same fierce and blunt and amazingly feminine stance I had noticed as a child.

"Isn't it nice," Santha said politely, "that Peter has had such a fine novel published at such a young age."

"How old are you?" Lillian said.

I muttered that I would be twenty-nine in three months.

"That's not young," Lillian said and walked out.

SHE was living in a brownstone then with Hammett, who wasn't well, and she didn't go out much. I called her whenever I could think of a good excuse, which wasn't often. I finished my second novel and did a play of my first. When the play was going to be produced on Broadway, I called Lillian to say I was on my way to an audition for actors, felt ignorant and wasn't sure how to handle it. "I'm not either," Lillian said. "All I can tell you is that a good cold reading generally means a bad actor. Don't look for a performance, look for a quality. And have yourself a good meal right afterwards," she added, and hung up before I could ask her to have it with me.

As soon as the audition was over, I went by myself to a small French restaurant on the West Side and had frogs' legs and too much wine. Lillian was right, the meal helped. Southern French cooking is as comforting as Southern American cooking if you're as cross-eyed as I was.

Food for the Self-Involved

FROGS' LEGS PIQUANTE

Serves 6

4 pounds frogs' legs, rinsed and patted dry
½ cup vegetable oil
2 teaspoons brown roux (page 112)
½ cup onions, minced
2 tablespoons green pepper, minced
2 tablespoons celery, minced
1 clove garlic, minced
4 cups tomatoes, peeled, seeded and chopped
2 tablespoons parsley, minced
2 tablespoons scallions, minced
salt and pepper

Season frogs' legs lightly with salt and pepper and fry in vegetable oil. Remove legs to a platter. Add brown roux to fat in the skillet, then add onions, green pepper, and celery. Cook 5 minutes. Add garlic, tomatoes and ½ teaspoon of salt. Cook for 5 minutes over medium heat. Add frogs' legs and baste to warm. Add parsley and scallions and serve.

A FEW years later, I don't remember exactly how many, I had taken a small house in Los Angeles and was working on a movie script when Dorothy Parker, who lived two houses down on the same block, told me one afternoon that she had heard Lillian was in town. I called a couple of hotels, found her at the Beverly Wilshire, and asked her to dinner.

When I went to pick her up, Lillian was standing over a vent in the floor. "I've never been as cold in my life as I am in Hollywood," she said. "They don't have any heat here. It's too sunny. What are we having for dinner?"

I said I had planned to take her to a restaurant that had been around a long time. "I hope it's good," Lillian said. "Nobody in this town likes food — except for fancy drek like Beef Wellington or Baked Alaska." I said I didn't like Beef Wellington, but I liked Baked Alaska about once every five years, the way I liked a banana split. "I wish you hadn't told me that," Lillian said, "I'm not sure I'd be having dinner with you. I've never been out with a man who liked Baked Alaska. It's no use saying you're sorry," she added, "you shouldn't have made the remark in the first place. It's very upsetting to me. New Orleans people are supposed to have some taste in food . . ."

She went on complaining about it till we got to the restaurant and had a quite decent meal. The dinner was to be the beginning of a series of meals stretching over more than two decades. Lillian and I have eaten together in San Francisco; New Orleans; New York; Boston; Connecticut; Sarasota; Palm Beach; three islands in the Caribbean; two yachts in different waters; Maine; Mexico; Paris; London; Rome; Cairo, and (for two weeks) floating down the Nile.

We often went somewhere to write, and we always found something to complain about. In San Francisco the lamb was overdone; in New Orleans the gumbo wasn't what it used to be; in New York the restaurant food was an expensive rip-off; in Boston the clam chowder had too much flour in it; in Connecticut the food was too rich; in Sarasota it was slipshod; in Palm Beach it was piss-elegant; in the Caribbean it was Caribbean; on the yachts it was cold; in Maine a lobster was stuffed instead of boiled; in Mexico food was greasy; in Paris everything had a sauce on it; in London nothing had a sauce on it; in Rome the pasta was lumpy, and in Cairo the food wasn't food.

After Hammett's death Lillian could travel whenever she wanted and we often met in this or that city for a week or two, prowling the local eating places for lunch and dinner. Her presence seldom went unnoticed. There's a hotel in Puerto Vallarta that will never be the same since the morning she tried to get a three-minute soft-boiled egg for breakfast. When the Mexican waiter was sent back down from the fourteenth floor to the kitchen for the third time, and it became apparent that he was going to kill her, I went into my room and swore never to translate anything else into Spanish for anybody, as long as I lived. Lillian said it was all right with her if I wanted to behave childishly and in the afternoon she went out by herself and bought a can of sardines, a can of tuna, some crackers and cheese—and one egg.

Lillian had a habit of setting up a small food supply in any hotel she visited, and she usually packed something that would boil water (a small electric pot or a metal coil) in case room service turned out to be what room service usually turns out to be.

Lillian likes soft-boiled eggs the way I do, with the white hard and the yolk soft, which is hard to achieve unless you know what you're doing.

The way you get that kind of egg is by putting cold water in a pot on the stove with the egg in it. Add a dash of vinegar (in case the shell cracks, to keep the egg white from streaking out) and turn the flame on. When the water heats to a full boil, start timing — not before. Then count 3 minutes, take the egg out and hold it under cold running water. If you're serving it in the shell, an egg cup is in order. If you're serving it out of the shell, break it into a small stem glass (a wineglass will do) with fresh ground pepper and salt if you like salt (Lillian does, I don't).

Do not make the mistake of thinking anybody can cook a boiled egg. Anybody can't.

The years we traveled (or met) in sundry parts of the world were like a chainlink of special occasions. We had fine times writing in whatever hemisphere, whatever city or country we found ourselves in, tumbling around the globe with portable electric typewriters that were often useless because of local electric current, cooking in hotels, going to local markets and discovering new places to eat. In Egypt, as guests of Max Palevsky, we met and ate on a boat he had chartered and played poker at night with his other friends. After Los Angeles, so vast in terms of space and so small in terms of time, Egypt was shockingly the opposite: vast in time and tiny in space, a thin ribbon of green on an empty desert. After poker one evening, I walked Lillian to her cabin and she opened her purse and took out some hard rolls, cold meat and whatever else she had stolen on the boat during the day. The thefts were unnecessary since Max provided everything we needed and would gladly have sent something to Lillian's cabin if he knew she wanted it. He didn't know. In the soft blue black of the Egyptian night, we sat outside the cabin surrounded by darkness and made cold midnight sandwiches.

ONE year I went back to New Orleans alone, and took an apartment for a while in the French Quarter. That was the year Lillian flew down from New York to keep me company, and one night we had dinner at Commander's Palace and both got drunk on something that Paul Prudhomme, who was still chef there, had invented, called a Cajun Martini. We recuperated for the next few days and then took to ordering Café Brûlot after dinner, with more or less the same effect. Café Brûlot, a blend of coffee, brandy, lemon peel and cloves, sometimes with cinnamon — all mixed together and flambéed — has long been a local Creole tradition. A silver brûlot bowl is not an uncommon wedding present in New Orelans, passed down from generation to generation. Flaming Café Brûlot makes a nice dramatic flourish at the end of a formal meal and it causes heat inside the body that holds through any winter night. In summer, a New Orleans friend once taught me to reverse things by chilling several glassfuls of crushed ice in the freezer and pouring the flambéed mixture into them at the last minute. Iced Café Brûlot does something indescribable and pleasing that lasts for hours. In New Orleans for some reason, if you substitute orange peel for lemon peel, the name is often changed to Café Diable.

Drinks for Special Occasions

CAJUN MARTINI

Serves many

2 jalapeña peppers
2 hot chili peppers
1 bottle vodka
1 bottle gin
dry vermouth to taste

Add 1 jalapeña and 1 hot chili pepper to bottle of vodka. Recap and store in freezer. Repeat process with bottle of gin. Mix a martini in the proportions you like. Serve ice cold and straight up garnished with a good green olive. The longer the bottles are refrigerated, the more fiery these martinis become.

CAFÉ BRÛLOT

Serves 4

1 cup cognac
¾ cup orange liqueur
7 cloves

peelings of 1 lemon, cut into thin strips
1 tablespoon sugar
1 cinnamon stick
2 cups espresso or strong black coffee

Combine cognac, orange liqueur, cloves, lemon peel, sugar and cinnamon stick in a chafing dish. Light the mixture with a match and stir while flaming for 1 minute. Add coffee and serve immediately.

ICED CAFÉ DIABLE

Serves 6

1 orange, cut into quarters
peel from 1 orange
15 cloves
2 sticks cinnamon
¼ cup sugar
4 cups fresh-brewed espresso
1 cup brandy
¼ cup orange liqueur

Combine quartered orange, orange peel, cloves, cinnamon, sugar and coffee in a pan over high heat. Flame with brandy and orange liqueur and serve over cracked ice.

In recent years, Lillian took to spending winters in Los Angeles where I bought a house with some money I made fixing a movie script for some producer. When I first visited Hollywood years ago, the town was run by the daughter of one of its former movie magnates who gave godawful dinners with too many waiters and the menu printed in gold on each plate. Food fashions have changed since then, and the new owners of Hollywood try to downplay its richness. What hasn't changed is the quality of the cooking. It's still godawful.

The last time I took Lillian to a Hollywood party she sat very politely through drinks and turned to me only once, chewing a canapé, to ask, with her usual delicacy and social aplomb, "What kind of rat-fuck am I eating?"

After that I figured there was no percentage in taking her to any private house in or around movieland, excepting those owned by Joan Didion and John Gregory Dunne, Sidney Pollack, President Goldberger of Cal Tech or the very few others who know about food.

Year before last (a few weeks after the summer Lillian asked what kind of food I ate growing up), I went back to Los Angeles alone to work on a novel and was at my typewriter when a call came saying that she was in trouble. She had been taken to Massachusetts General Hospital in Boston and was facing two lengthy surgical procedures.

I spent the next three months in Boston. From my hotel window across the river I could see Lillian's window, and sometimes in the evenings they let me take her out in a wheelchair by taxi to a restaurant. Hospital food being what it is, any complaints about cooking she voiced up to then faded into a dim memory. At least one hospital dietician will never be the same, and three night nurses said they had never heard language like that in their lives.

After the first surgery Lillian smuggled a salt cellar into the hospital and hid it under her mattress. Soon after that they let me take her out again for an occasional dinner and by the end of the second month it seemed clear that the anticipation of a decent meal was good for this particular patient even if the patient couldn't get the meal down.

Food for a Hospital Patient

PASTA PENTIMENTO

Serves 4

1 pound vermicelli
12 anchovy filets, minced

6 cloves garlic, minced
2 tablespoons sun-dried tomatoes, minced
½ cup good olive oil
½ teaspoon chili pepper
½ teaspoon coarsely ground black pepper
½ cup grated Parmesan cheese

Begin to boil a pot of water for the pasta. Heat olive oil, add anchovies, garlic, sun-dried tomatoes, chili pepper and black pepper. Cook over high heat until garlic begins to turn golden. Remove from heat. Cook and drain pasta. Toss pasta with sauce, adding Parmesan cheese as you toss. Turn out on a warm platter or pasta bowls, and garnish with additional anchovy filets.

PASTA WITH MUSSELS, MUSHROOMS AND CREAM

Serves 4

1 pound fettucine
3 pounds mussels, cleaned and debearded
1 cup dry white wine
1 cup water
1 shallot, finely minced
2 cups mushrooms, thinly sliced
4 tablespoons butter
½ pint heavy cream
½ cup chopped parsley
kosher salt and coarsely ground black pepper

Steam mussels in wine and water. Drain, reserve cooking liquid, and allow to cool. Melt butter and soften shallot and mushrooms over low heat. Season lightly with salt and pepper, cooking mushrooms until very soft. Meanwhile, pick the mussels and put a large pot of water on to boil for pasta. When mushrooms are soft, add one cup of reserved mussel broth and ½ pint of heavy cream. Reduce to a coating consistency, add mussels, and adjust seasoning with kosher salt and coarsely ground black pepper. Boil pasta until al dente, drain well and toss in sauce with chopped parsley. Turn out on a warm platter or pasta bowls.

PAN-FRIED SOFTSHELL CRABS

Serves 6

12 softshell crabs, cleaned
2 cups milk
dash of hot sauce
4 cups flour, seasoned with salt and pepper
2 cups drawn (clarified) butter
2 lemons, quartered
1 cup dry white wine
½ cup parsley, minced

Combine milk and hot sauce. Soak the crabs for 15 minutes in this mixture. Cover the bottom of a heavy skillet with about ¼ inch of drawn butter. Dust the crabs in seasoned flour and fry two at a time over medium heat until golden (usually about 5 minutes on the first side and 3 minutes on the second side). Remove to a warm platter. When all the crabs are fried, discard the frying butter. Squeeze lemon wedges into the pan, add wine, and scrape vigorously. Add parsley and continue cooking sauce for 3 minutes. Adjust seasoning with salt and pepper. Drizzle sauce over crabs and serve immediately with additional lemon wedges.

DUMPLING SOUP

Serves 6

SOUP:
4 tablespoons goose fat
2 parsnips, peeled and julienned
3 carrots
6 pearl onions
1 teaspoon sage
1 teaspoon thyme
1 clove
8 cups goose or chicken stock
4 cups leftover goose or goose confit cut into small pieces
kosher salt and black pepper

Melt goose fat in a large pot and add parsnips, carrots, onions, sage, thyme and clove. Cook over low heat until onions begin to caramelize. Add stock and simmer until carrots are tender. Add meat.

SPONGE DUMPLINGS:
1 cup all-purpose flour
½ teaspoon kosher salt
pinch of nutmeg
1 cup boiling water
2 eggs
1 teaspoon goose fat

Combine flour, salt and nutmeg. Add boiling water to flour mixture and beat vigorously. Add eggs one at a time, beating batter well. When smooth, add goose fat.

TO ASSEMBLE SOUP:

Strain the soup and reserve vegetables and meat on a warm platter. Put soup on to boil and drop in dumpling mixture by the tablespoon. Reduce heat and simmer for 5 minutes. Add vegetables and serve.

WHEN the three months were up and Lillian's comments on hospital cuisine had begun to escalate, the doctors gave up and she was declared well enough to leave Boston and go home to New York by ambulance. By then her room at Mass General looked like a small bar-and-grill surrounded by Intensive Care equipment. Her secretary and friend, Rita Wade, aided by a trained nurse, packed up the cans of food, boxes of crackers, tins of cheese and wine bottles, and hung them in sacks from her hospital bed. A cheer went up from the nurses' station as they wheeled Lillian into the waiting ambulance.

I went along for the ride, which made it the second time we had been in an ambulance together (the first was in San Francisco when we both had a lecture to give in Marin and Lillian hurt her back). The ride from Boston to New York took nearly seven hours, not including one twenty-minute respite when I broke my promise about fast-food diners and stopped at one for a cheeseburger and a chocolate malt. The cheeseburger was for me and the chocolate malt was for Lillian, who was in considerable discomfort, though not enough not to keep up a running commentary on the sad state of Jews in America as exemplified by my desire to put a slice of cheese together with chopped meat between a bun and eat it. I happen to like cheeseburgers, which Lillian considered a kind of fetish. It gave us something to argue about for the rest of the ride.

Food for an Ambulance

CHICKEN SANDWICHES

6 sandwiches

1 roast tarragon chicken (see page 152)
¼ cup homemade mayonnaise (see page 27)
12 slices Pepperidge Farm bread, crust removed

Slice breast meat very thin. Cover each slice of bread with mayonnaise and layer chicken slices on one half. Season meat lightly with salt and pepper, cover with second slice of bread. Slice in half diagonally and wrap well for ambulance ride.

RESTORATIVE BROTH

1 gallon

1 fowl
1 smoked ham hock
2 turkey wings
1 head garlic
1 onion
2 jalepeña peppers
2 bay leaves

1 tablespoon black peppercorns
1 teaspoon salt
juice from two lemons

Combine fowl, smoked ham hock, turkey wings, garlic, onion, peppers, bay leaves, black peppercorns and salt in a large pot with 2 gallons of cold water. Simmer for 3 hours, then strain and chill. Remove fat. Heat soup. Add lemon juice and store soup in a thermos for ambulance ride.

It took Lillian several months to recuperate from the surgery and I stayed in New York for as long as I could. We ate our meals together and I lost weight while she gained: the same food served both purposes. The only thing Lillian asked for repeatedly was the dish she had eaten as a child whenever she was in trouble. She said she had called it "Cheese-Mac" when she was five years old and she called it "Cheese-Mac" now.

Food for Recovery

MACARONI AND CHEESE

Serves 6

1 pound macaroni
1 tablespoon honey
2 teaspoons pepper
½ pound bacon, cut into ¼-inch pieces
1 pound cheddar cheese, grated
3 tomatoes, sliced
1 cup milk
1 cup cream

Preheat oven to 350 degrees. Boil macaroni in plenty of water with 1 tablespoon of honey. Drain and cool under cold water. Layer one-third of the macaroni, then half of the bacon, one-third of the macaroni, then half of the cheese. Add the remaining macaroni, another layer of bacon, a layer of the remaining cheese, and then a layer of sliced tomatoes. Combine milk and cream and pour over casserole. Bake at 350 degrees for 30 minutes until cheese is melted.

DIET CHICKEN MARINADE

Serves 6

2 chickens, cut into parts and skinned
juice of 1 lemon
½ cup white wine
3 cloves garlic, crushed
1 onion, sliced
2 tablespoons fresh ginger, chopped
1 bunch fresh dill, chopped
1 teaspoon salt
1 teaspoon oregano
1 teaspoon thyme
¼ teaspoon allspice

Preheat oven to 400 degrees. Combine lemon, wine, garlic, onion, ginger, dill, salt, oregano, thyme and allspice in a large casserole. Add chicken and allow to marinate for 3 hours, turning each piece several times. Place casserole in oven and bake chicken in marinade 45 minutes until done.

EGGPLANT SOUFFLÉ

Serves 6

3 medium-size eggplants, cut into cubes
6 tablespoons butter
¼ cup chopped onion
1 clove garlic, minced
¾ cup Parmesan cheese, grated
1 cup milk
3 tablespoons flour
4 eggs, separated
2 tablespoons tomato paste
¼ teaspoon cayenne papper
1 teaspoon salt

Preheat oven to 375 degrees. Steam eggplant in water for 25 minutes. Drain. Puree in blender and transfer to a sieve to extract all liquid. Sauté onion and garlic in 4 tablespoons of butter until soft. Combine flour and milk and whisk until smooth. Add milk to onion mixture and cook over low heat for 3 minutes. Remove from heat. Beat 4 egg yolks and add several tablespoons of warm onion sauce to warm the yolks. Then combine the yolks with the sauce. Add tomato paste, cayenne pepper, ½ cup grated Parmesan, salt and eggplant puree to the onion and egg yolk mixture and set aside. Beat egg whites until stiff and fold into eggplant mixture. Coat a 4-quart soufflé dish with 2 tablespoons of butter and ¼ cup of Parmesan. Pour eggplant mixture into soufflé dish and bake at 375 degrees for 30 to 40 minutes, until it puffs up.

DIET BISCUITS

6 biscuits

2 tablespoons cooking oil
1 cup stone ground white cornmeal
2 teaspoons baking powder
1 egg, separated
¾ cup milk

Preheat oven to 400 degrees. Brush a muffin tin with 1 tablespoon of the oil. Combine baking soda and cornmeal. Combine milk, egg yolk and 1 tablespoon of oil. Blend this mixture with the baking powder and cornmeal mixture. Whip the egg white until stiff. Fold into batter. Pour into muffin tins (each cup should be half full). Bake in 400-degree oven 15 to 20 minutes until done.

BEEF STEW

Serves 6

1½ pounds round steak, cut into bite-size pieces
2 cups flour
1 teaspoon salt
½ teaspoon pepper
bacon or salt pork

1 onion, chopped
1 clove garlic, minced
bay leaf
1 teaspoon thyme
1 teaspoon oregano
2 cups white wine
2 tablespoons liquid espresso coffee
½ cup parsley, chopped
4 carrots, peeled and cut into bite-size pieces

Preheat oven to 300 degrees. Combine flour, salt and pepper in a brown paper bag. Add cut round steak and shake to dust each piece. Discard excess flour. Put salt pork or bacon in a large casserole over medium heat and render the fat. Increase heat, add beef, and brown on all sides. Reduce heat and add onion and garlic. Cook slowly until onion is wilted. Add bay leaf, thyme, oregano, white wine and espresso and bring stew to a boil. Cover the casserole and place in 300-degree oven for one hour. Add carrots and parsley, stir, return to oven and cook for 30 additional minutes. Serve over warm egg noodles.

A FEW months later I was back in Los Angeles when Lillian called from New York to say that she had decided to come out for a visit. She wanted to know what I thought. I said I thought it was a crazy idea.

Three weeks later she arrived by plane on a stretcher with a trained nurse, a young doctor named Jonathan La Pook who had befriended her, several suitcases of clothes, two of medications — and a Virginia ham. The ham was a present to me. It meant she wanted me to cook red beans.

At this writing, Lillian is again spending the winter in Los Angeles. A hospital bed has been rented for her and she is ensconced in the guest wing of a friend whose house is big enough to accommodate her and the nurses. She needs the nurses because she is legally blind, partially paralyzed and virtually unable to walk.

"I'm no fun anymore," she said several months ago, trying to sit up in bed. After a long pause she added: "But I *was* fun. Wasn't I?"

I was reading a book by the window and asked her to shut up till I finished the page I was on.

"I'll shut up," Lillian said, "on one condition. When we talk, we talk about something important."

"Such as?" I said.

"Such as," Lillian said, "what are we having for dinner?"

POSTSCRIPT
Martha's Vineyard, July 4, 1984

FIVE days ago, on June 29, Lillian died, here on Martha's Vineyard. I was to have visited her on the fifteenth of July.

The afternoon of her death, I phoned her from Los Angeles to say I'd be a little late because the galley proofs of this book, which I was bringing to read to her, had been delayed.

"You *can't* be late," Lillian said. I told her it was only a matter of a couple of days. "You don't understand," Lillian said, "I want to work, I want to work, I want to work."

She said it three times. It's the last thing I remember her saying, and she died six hours later.

A couple of months ago I had gone to see her in New York for what was to be the last time. She had by then taken to putting my name down as next of kin on all hospital and medical records. I think she did that just to annoy me. It caused doctors and nurses to tell me, with relentless regularity, everything that went wrong with her — most of which I didn't want to hear because there was nothing I could do about it.

When I walked into her New York apartment that day, there was a replacement nurse I hadn't met who collared me in the hall. "Miss Hellman," she said, "is paralyzed, blind and having rage attacks. She can't help the rage attacks, which are the result of her strokes, and she can't sleep. She can't eat. She can't walk. She can't find a comfortable spot in the hospital bed that's been provided for her, or in an easy chair, or on a sofa, or any place in her life. She's weaker today than she was yesterday, her memory is beginning to fade, and frankly I think she's dying."

I thanked her for the information and went in to Lillian. "How are you?" I said.

"Not good, Peter," Lillian said.

I asked why not.

"This is the worst case of writer's block I ever had in my life," Lillian said. "*The* worst case."

The perception of her own demise as writer's block is all I can think of now to say about Lillian, and it was all I could think of at her funeral yesterday. "Here lies a lady with writer's block" was all there was to say.

After the funeral some of her friends came back to her house on the Vineyard and I tried, with John and Barbara Hersey, to see that there was some food around more or less the way Lillian would have spread it.

I have no idea whether we did it right, but we did our best.

Index

Index

About the Authors

LILLIAN HELLMAN was born in New Orleans, spent her childhood between New Orleans and New York, attended New York University and Columbia. In 1934 she launched her career as a playwright with *The Children's Hour*. Over the next three decades came a succession of major achievements in the theater, among them *The Little Foxes, Watch on the Rhine, Another Part of the Forest, The Autumn Garden,* and *Toys in the Attic*. Miss Hellman twice was the recipient of the New York Drama Critics Circle Award for the best play of the year *(Watch on the Rhine* and *Toys in the Attic)*. In 1972 a definitive edition of all her work for the theater was published as *The Collected Plays*.

Miss Hellman's memoir *An Unfinished Woman* was published in 1969 and was the winner of the National Book Award. It was followed in 1973 by *Pentimento,* in 1976 by *Scoundrel Time,* and in 1980 by *Maybe*.

Miss Hellman lived in New York City and Martha's Vineyard before her death in 1984.

PETER FEIBLEMAN was born in New Orleans, spent his childhood between New Orleans and New York, attended Carnegie Institute of Technology and Columbia. His first novel, *A Place without Twilight,* was published in 1958 to wide critical acclaim and won him a Guggenheim Fellowship for creative writing. Since then he has written three other novels, *The Daughters of Necessity, The Columbus Tree,* and *Charlie Boy,* a Broadway play, *Tiger, Tiger Burning Bright,* a book of four novellas entitled *Strangers and Graves,* and numerous stories and articles. For many years has traveled, lived in, and written about Spain. He lives in Los Angeles and Martha's Vineyard.